SHEPHERD'S NOTES

SHEPHERD'S NOTES

When you need a guide through the Scriptures

I *Corinthians*

BROADMAN
&HOLMAN
PUBLISHERS

Nashville, Tennessee

Shepherd's Notes—*1 Corinthians*
© 1998
by Broadman & Holman Publishers
Nashville, Tennessee
All rights reserved
Printed in the United States of America

Dewey Decimal Classification: 227.207
Subject Heading: BIBLE N.T. CORINTHIANS
Library of Congress Card Catalog Number: 98–27585

Library of Congress Cataloging-in-Publication Data

Gould, Dana, 1951–
1 Corinthians/ Dana Gould, editor
        p. cm.   — (Shepherd's notes)
    Includes bibliographical references.
    ISBN 0–8054–9325–5 (trade paper)
        1. Bible. N.T. Corinthians, 1st—Study and teaching. I. Title.   II. Series.
BS2675.5.G67   1998
227'.207—dc21

                                                                98–27585
                                                                          CIP

1 2 3 4 5 6   03 02 01 00 99 98

CONTENTS

Dear Reader:

Shepherd's Notes are designed to give you a quick, step-by-step overview of every book of the Bible. They are not meant to be substitutes for the biblical text; rather, they are study guides intended to help you explore the wisdom of Scripture in personal or group study and to apply that wisdom successfully in your own life.

Shepherd's Notes guide you through the main themes of each book of the Bible and illuminate fascinating details through appropriate commentary and reference notes. Historical and cultural background information bring the Bible into sharper focus.

Six different icons, used throughout the series, call your attention to historical-cultural information, Old Testament and New Testament references, word pictures, unit summaries, and personal application for everyday life.

Whether you are a novice or a veteran at Bible study, I believe you will find *Shepherd's Notes* a resource that will take you to a new level in your mining and applying the riches of Scripture.

In Him,

David R. Shepherd
Editor-in-Chief

HOW TO USE THIS BOOK

DESIGNED FOR THE BUSY USER

Shepherd's Notes for 1 Corinthians is designed to provide an easy-to-use tool for getting a quick handle on this Bible book's important features, and for gaining an understanding of the message of 1 Corinthians. Information available in more difficult-to-use reference works has been incorporated into the *Shepherd's Notes* format. This brings you the benefits of many more advanced and expensive works packed into one small volume.

Shepherd's Notes are for laymen, pastors, teachers, small-group leaders and participants, as well as the classroom student. Enrich your personal study or quiet time. Shorten your class or small-group preparation time as you gain valuable insights into the truths of God's Word that you can pass along to your students or group members.

DESIGNED FOR QUICK ACCESS

Bible students with time constraints will especially appreciate the time-saving features built in *Shepherd's Notes*. All features are intended to aid a quick and concise encounter with the heart of the message of this New Testament book.

Concise Commentary. Short sections provide quick "snapshots" of passages, highlighting important points and other information.

Outlined Text. A comprehensive outline covers the entire text of 1 Corinthians. This is a valuable feature for following the narrative's flow, allowing for a quick, easy way to locate a particular passage.

Shepherd's Notes. These summary statements appear at the close of every key section of the narrative. While functioning in part as a quick summary, they also deliver the essence of the message presented in the sections they cover.

Icons. Various icons in the margin highlight recurring themes in 1 Corinthians, aiding in selective searching or tracing of those themes.

Sidebars and Charts. These specially selected features provide additional background information to your study or preparation. These include definitions as well as cultural, historical, and biblical insights.

Maps. These are placed at appropriate places in the book to aid your understanding and study of a text or passage.

Questions to Guide Your Study. These thought-provoking questions and discussion starters are designed to encourage interaction with the truth and principles of God's Word.

In addition to the above features, study aids have been included at the back of the book for those readers who require or desire more information and resources for working through 1 Corinthians. These include chapter outlines for studying 1 Corinthians and a list of reference sources used for this volume which offer many works that allow the reader to extend the scope of his or her study of this letter.

DESIGNED TO WORK FOR YOU

Personal Study. Using the *Shepherd's Notes* with a passage of Scripture can enlighten your study and take it to a new level. At your fingertips is information that would require searching several volumes to find. In addition, many points of application occur throughout the volume, contributing to personal growth.

Teaching. Outlines frame the text of 1 Corinthians, providing a logical presentation of the message. Shepherd's Notes provide summary statements for presenting the essence of key points and events. Personal Application icons point out personal application of the message of 1 Corinthians, and Historical Context icons indicate where background information is supplied.

Group Study. Shepherd's Notes can be an excellent companion volume to use for gaining a quick but accurate understanding of the message of a Bible book. Each group member can benefit by having his or her own copy. The *Notes* format accommodates the study of or the tracing of the themes throughout 1 Corinthians. Leaders may use its flexible features to prepare for group sessions, or use during group sessions. Questions to Guide Your Study can spark discussion of the key points and truths of 1 Corinthians.

LIST OF MARGIN ICONS USED IN 1 CORINTHIANS

 Shepherd's Notes. Placed at the end of each section, a capsule statement provides the reader with the essence of the message of that section.

 Historical Context. To indicate background information—historical, biographical, cultural—and provide insight on the understanding or interpretation of a passage.

 Old Testament Reference. To indicate an Old Testament passage that illuminates a passage in 1 Corinthians.

 New Testament Reference. Used when the writer refers to New Testament passages that are either fulfilled prophecy, an antitype of an Old Testament type, or a New Testament text which in some other way illuminates the passages under discussion.

 Personal Application. Used when the text provides a personal or universal application of truth.

 Word Picture. Indicates that the meaning of a specific word or phrase is illustrated so as to shed light on it.

For Paul's most complete statement of the gospel of God's grace, we must turn to Romans. But for his most extensive correspondence with a single church, we must turn to the Corinthian letters.

Here a number of his converts struggled with the responsibility of being the people of God in the midst of a pagan city. Some of them had been saved out of lifestyles marked by gross sin (6:9–11), and the temptation to lapse into old vices remained strong. They all lived under the relentless pressures of a pagan society which sought to conform them to its corrupt ways. Thus, 1 Corinthians provides the most intimate disclosure of the inner life and workings of an early congregation to be found in the New Testament.

FIRST CORINTHIANS IN A "NUTSHELL"

Purpose:	To answer the Corinthians' questions and to restore their areas of weakness
Major Themes:	Christian wisdom, sexual immorality, marriage and divorce, spiritual gifts, women in the church, the Lord's Supper, and the Resurrection

AUTHOR

The letter (1:1, 2; 16–21) as well as church tradition acknowledge Paul as the author of 1 Corinthians. This affirmation generally has gone unchallenged.

The Apostle Paul

Paul is the official name of this outstanding missionary apostle. (Paul's Jewish name was Saul.) He was born on Turkey's southern shore in Tarsus. Well trained in Jewish Scriptures and tradition, he also learned the trade of tentmaking. He is the author of many New Testament epistles.

Paul's third missionary journey centered in Ephesus, from which the gospel probably spread into the surrounding cities. From Ephesus he carried on a correspondence with the Corinthian church. While in Corinth at the end of this journey, he wrote his epistle to the Romans.

PURPOSE FOR WRITING

Paul dealt with several problems in this letter. He learned of these matters through the report from Chloe's people (1:11), common rumors (5:1), and from information received from the church (7:1; 8:1; 12:1; 16:1). Paul wrote to answer the questions the Corinthians had put to him, but he had other concerns as well. Although the church was quite gifted (1:4–7), it was equally immature and unspiritual (3:1–4). Paul wanted to restore the church in its areas of weakness. Through the inspiration of the Holy Spirit, he articulated the New Testament's clearest exposition of the Lord's Supper, the Resurrection, and spiritual gifts.

*Problems Reflected in 1 Corinthians**

PROBLEM	PASSAGE
Factions	1:10–17; 3:5–15
Worldly Wisdom	1:18–31; 2:6–3:4
Unethical Conduct	5:1–6:20
Marriage and Celibacy	7:1–40
Idols	8:1–11:2
Actions of Women Leaders	11:3–16
Lord's Supper	11:17–34
Spiritual Gifts	12:1–14:40
Unbelief in the Resurrection	15:1–58

*Chart taken from Joe Blair, *Introducing the New Testament*, p. 155.

DATE OF WRITING

According to 1 Corinthians 16:8, 9, Paul was in Ephesus when he wrote this letter. Although we are not able to date this letter with great precision, we can be reasonably accurate if we date it A.D. 54 or 55.

A CHRONOLOGY OF PAUL'S RELATIONSHIP WITH THE CORINTHIAN CHURCH*

1. Paul evangelized Corinth during his second journey (Acts 18:1–11).

2. Paul wrote a letter to Corinth, now lost, in which he urged Christians to avoid association with professing believers who were immoral (1 Cor. 5:9–11).

3. Paul wrote 1 Corinthians from Ephesus during his third missionary journey to advise the Corinthians on handling problems in the church.

4. Paul made a "painful" visit to Corinth from Ephesus to correct problems in the church. His visit failed to achieve its aim (2 Cor. 2:1).

5. Paul sent another letter, also lost, calling the Corinthians to repentance and urging discipline for an opponent in the church (2 Cor. 2:4–11). Titus carried the letter to Corinth. Scholars have named this letter the "severe" letter.

6. Paul left Ephesus, for Troas, and then to Macedonia, to await word on the success of Titus's visit (2 Cor. 2:12, 13).

7. Titus met Paul in Macedonia with the report of the Corinthian church's warm acceptance of Paul's letter and eagerness to see him (2 Cor. 7:5–16).

8. Paul wrote 2 Corinthians from Macedonia and sent it to Corinth by Titus.

9. Paul went to Corinth for his third visit (2 Cor. 12:14; 13:1; Acts 20:2).

*List taken from Thomas D. Lea, *The New Testament: Its Background and Message*, p. 412.

AUDIENCE

The church at Corinth was a picture of converts who had come out of the environment and culture of the city of Corinth. The church had several problems, among them a leadership problem producing divisions in the church (1:10–17). Immoral practices were not being dealt with (5:1–6:20). An enthusiastic group in the church flaunted their spiritual gifts (12:1–14:40). A legalistic group was concerned about dietary laws (8:1–10:32). Some were abusing the Lord's Supper (11:17–34), and others were offering false teachings regarding the Resurrection (15:1–58). These matters—in addition to its multiethnic makeup of Greeks, Romans, and Jews and a mixture of social classes including rich, poor, and slave—made for a unique and troubled congregation.

THE DOCTRINES OF 1 CORINTHIANS

The focus of 1 Corinthians is not on doctrinal theology but pastoral theology. This letter deals with:

- the problem of those who bring division to the body of Christ (1:11–3:4);
- the treatment of fellow Christians who sin (5:1–13);
- matters of sexuality in marriage and divorce (7:1–40);
- propriety in church worship (11:2–34); and
- disputes about food (8:1–11:1).

THE THEOLOGICAL SIGNIFICANCE AND RELEVANCE OF 1 CORINTHIANS

If Paul were to write a letter to the average church today, he probably would rewrite much of 1 Corinthians. The Corinthians' world was much like our modern world. The people had the same thirst for intellectualism, the same moral permissiveness, and certainly the same fascination for the spectacular. The church resembled our churches—extremely proud, affluent, and fiercely eager for acceptance by the world.

In doctrine, there existed a mixture of truth and error. In ethics, the church manifested widespread immorality and worldliness. Two valuable contributions come from this letter. First, we have the doctrinal and pastoral expositions of the topics discussed. Second, we have Paul's practical counsel for living as Christians in a pagan society. Paul carefully defined each issue and then offered helpful principles to deal with them. What we learn from the apostle's method is as important for the contemporary church as the solutions he articulated.

BASIC OUTLINE FOR 1 CORINTHIANS

    I. Introduction (1:1–9)

    II. Concerning Divisions (1:10–3:4)

    III. Concerning Leadership (3:5–4:21)

    IV. Concerning Immorality (5:1–6:20)

    V. Concerning Marriage (7:1–40)

    VI. Concerning Food Offered to Idols (8:1–11:1)

    VII. Concerning Orderly Worship (11:2–34)

    VIII. Concerning Spiritual Gifts (12:1–14:40)

    IX. Concerning the Resurrection (15:1–58)

    X. Concerning the Collection and Closing Remarks (16:1–24)

QUESTIONS TO GUIDE YOUR STUDY

    1. Who were Paul's readers? Why did he write to them?

    2. What problems did Paul address at Corinth?

    3. What are the key doctrines Paul addressed in this letter?

    4. What make his message relevant to today's readers?

The City of Corinth

The city of Corinth was located on a narrow strip of land that connected the Peloponnesian Peninsula with northern Greece. It had two seaports, Cenchrea on the Aegean side in the east and Lechaeum at the edge of the gulf of Corinth in the west. The city's location made it a crossroads for travel and commerce and contributed to its prosperity. Ship captains, eager to avoid the stormy dangers of sailing around the Peloponnesian Straits on the south, would dock at one port of Corinth. Their cargo was unloaded, hauled overland, and then loaded in another vessel in port on the opposite side. They avoided the risk of losing ships and lives in the dangerous voyage along the southern route.

Corinth was also known for hosting athletic events known as the Isthmian games. These events took place every two years. Huge crowds thronged to the city for the festivities.

Paul's Lists of Spiritual Gifts[*]

Spiritual Gift	Rom. 12:6–8	1 Cor. 12:8–10	1 Cor. 12:28	1 Cor. 12:29–30	Eph. 4:11
Apostle			1	1	1
Prophet	1	5	2	2	2
Teacher	3		3	3	5
Pastor					4
Miracles		4	4	4	
Discernment of Spirits		6			
Word of Wisdom, Knowledge		1			
Evangelists					3
Encouragers	4	4			
Faith		2			
Healings		3	5	5	
Tongues		7	8	6	
Interpretation		8		7	
Ministry/ Serving	2				
Administration			7		
Leaders	6				
Helpers			6		
Mercy	7				
Giving	5				

*Chart presents the order in which the gifts listed appear in the passage.

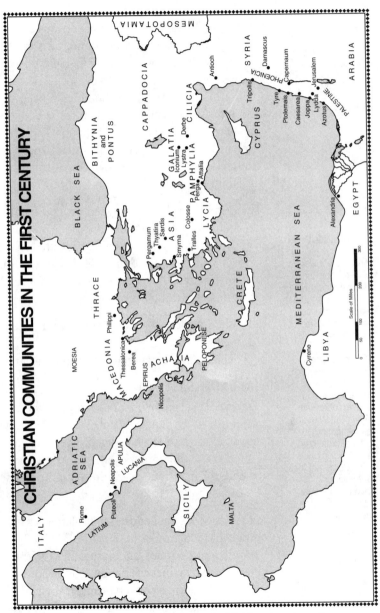

Taken from Kurt A. Richardson, *James*, vol. 36, New American Commentary (Nashville, Tenn. Broadman & Holman Publishers), 20.

1 CORINTHIANS 1

Paul visited Corinth on his second missionary journey and began teaching immediately in the synagogue there. Some of the Jews believed, but leaders and others rejected his witness. He continued his ministry in the home of a believer, Titius Justus, a Gentile who lived next door to the synagogue (Acts 18:7). Although Paul met resistance, his work went well, and a struggling church began with even the synagogue ruler and his family becoming Christians (Acts 18:7, 8).

The Corinthian church, plagued with problems, needed Paul's firm guidance. The problems with which they were struggling presented challenges to the nature and unity of the church. In this first part of his letter, chapter 1, Paul; addresses two of their problems:

- the challenge of factions within their church, and
- believers' fascination with worldly wisdom.

GREETINGS (1:1–3)

Writer (v. 1). The writer of 1 Corinthians identifies himself as the apostle Paul. This affirmation generally has gone unchallenged. The letter was written some time around A.D. 54 or 55, near the end of Paul's three-year ministry in Ephesus (1 Cor. 16:5–9; Acts 20:31).

Recipients (v. 2). Paul addresses his letter "to the church of God in Corinth" (v. 2). The city of Corinth, an important city of trade, had a reputation for wickedness. The church at Corinth was Gentile, and its converts came from a wide variety of backgrounds and religious experiences. These members had little, if any, preparation for living the Christian life, unlike other

The Hellenistic Letter

Generally, Paul's epistles follow the normal pattern of the hellenistic letter, the basic form of which consists of five major sections:

1. Opening (sender, addressee, greeting);

2. Thanksgiving or blessing (often with prayer of intercession, well wishes, or personal greetings);

3. The Burden of the letter (including citation of classical sources and arguments);

4. Parenesis (ethical instruction, exhortation); and

5. Closing (mention of personal plans, mutual friends, benediction).

churches that were made up of God-fearers, proselytes, and Jewish converts. In addressing the believers at Corinth, Paul had to deal with basic moral, church, and doctrinal matters.

We see a few notable expansions on the standard salutation:

1. *Paul identified himself as one whom God called "to be an apostle of Christ Jesus"* (v. 1). Paul did not choose the vocation to which he was called of God. Rather, it was a divine summons that he obeyed.

2. *Paul designated his readers as "the church of God in Corinth"* (v. 2). The word *church* comes from a word made up of two words: "out of" and "a calling." It refers to a body of people who have been "called out" and gathered for God's purposes. They are those who, through faith in Jesus Christ, have been separated unto God. They belong to God and are at His disposal.

3. *Paul magnified the grace and peace of God in his prayer for the Corinthian believers* (v. 3). The two qualities—peace and grace—sum up the essence of the Christian gospel. *Grace* is the unmerited favor of God and the expression of His love that we could never deserve. *Peace* is the consequence of God's grace in the lives of those who confess Jesus Christ as Lord.

Paul's opening greeting to his readers contains some expansions on the standard salutation. He makes reference to his vocation as an apostle—a divine summons that he obeyed. He describes his readers as a "church," those who have been sanctified and called to be separated unto God.

THANKSGIVING (1:4–9)

A customary feature of the hellenistic letter was thanksgiving. As with the address and prayer, it preceded the main body of the letter.

Thanking God for the Corinthians (v. 4)

Paul knew that he must address some tough problems at Corinth. He began with a word of

What can we learn from Paul's initial approach with the Corinthians as we are called upon to deal with problems in the church, at home, or in the workplace?

Facts About the Church

TERM	EXPANDED MEANING
A called-out group of people	The church is a group of people gathered together for a specific reason.
"Sanctified"	The church is separated unto God for His purposes.

affirmation—expressing what was right in the church. Paul thanked God for the evidence of His work among the Corinthians.

Paul's Readers Enriched in Every Way (vv. 5, 6)
The effect of God's grace in the Corinthian church was seen in their gifts of speaking and knowledge. Both of these endowments from God were given so the Corinthian believers would not be lacking (see 1 Cor. 12:8; 13:1, 2). But both gifts were subject to abuse in the church.

It seems that Paul anticipated that this event would occur in his own lifetime (1 Cor. 15:51, 52; 1 Thess. 4:16, 17). This would explain his statement that the Corinthians were eagerly awaiting "the revelation of our Lord Jesus Christ" (1 Cor. 1:7, NASB).

The Gifts Bestowed on the Corinthian Believers

GIFT OF GRACE	PURPOSE
"In all your speaking"	for the telling of the truth
"In all your knowledge"	for one's grasp of the truth

Anticipating the Lord's Return (vv. 7, 8)
Early Christians believed not only that Jesus Christ had died for their sins and had risen from the dead, but that He would soon return triumphantly in glory.

Paul assured (v. 8) this gifted, expectant congregation that Christ would provide what they needed to strengthen and sustain them to the very end. When they appear before Him, they will be blameless. This theme appears elsewhere in Paul's New Testament writings (see Rom. 5:9–11; 8:31–39).

The Fellowship of Christ (v. 9)

The remarkable hope Paul expressed in verse 8 rests upon a sure foundation, namely, the faithfulness of God. He is its unfailing guarantee. The word *fellowship* describes sharing with Christ. It refers to participation and communion. The call of God is a call to relationship and participation in the life of His Son.

Paul's salutation, in these first nine verses of chapter 1, reveals many aspects of God's call to us in Jesus Christ, as the following chart shows.

REVELATION ABOUT GOD'S CALL	VERSE
1. It sets us apart for God, making us saints.	v. 2
2. It relates us to the vibrant community of those in every place who call upon the name of Christ.	v. 2
3. It is an expression of God's grace and brings peace.	v. 3
4. It always enriches and endows us.	vv. 5, 7
5. It is mediated through testimony borne to Christ.	v. 6
6. It plants a sustaining hope and assures an ultimate deliverance.	vv. 7, 8
7. It rests upon the faithfulness of God and invites us to share in the life of Christ.	v. 9

"Eagerly await"

This phrase is only one word in the Greek text, and is an interesting compound consisting of three words. It is made up of two prefixed prepositions "from" and "out of" and the verb "to wait for." It means "to await or expect eagerly," "to anxiously await," and "to wait eagerly but patiently for something. . . . The double preposition in compound implies a degree of earnestness and intensity of expectation. . . . The present tense emphasizes the continuous action and the participle expresses an attendant circumstance" (Fritz Rienecker, *Linguistic Key to the Greek New Testament* [Grand Rapids: Zondervan, 1980], 386).

THE REPORT FROM CORINTH (1:10–17)

Following his affirmation of the Corinthians, Paul directed his attention (1:1–4:21) to the problem of divisions in the church. Not only did he address these divisions at the outset; he dealt with them at greater length than any other

Paul began his letter in the customary fashion, using the normal pattern of the Hellenistic letter: a greeting, a salutation, and a lengthy expression of his thanksgiving for the Corinthian believers. In his thanksgiving prayer, he offered thanks for their reception of the gospel, their giftedness, and particularly for God's faithfulness.

issue except the charismatic error in chapters 12–14.

Quarreling Among the Corinthians (vv. 10–12)

How did Paul know about the conflict among the Corinthians? Members of Chloe's household had told Paul about what was taking place. The New Testament reveals little about Chloe, but she was well enough known to give validity to Paul's source of information.

In verse 12, Paul specified the division or factions within the Corinthian church: "I follow Paul"; "I follow Apollos"; "I follow Cephas"; "I follow Christ."

Three Probing Questions (v. 13)

Paul responded to this rivalry by asking three rhetorical questions. Paul's purpose for these questions was not to receive information from his readers, but rather to make strong affirmations.

Paul's Probing Questions

QUESTION	AFFIRMATION
1. "Is Christ divided?"	Christ is *not* one among many.
2. "Was Paul crucified for you?"	*Only* Christ can atone for sin.
3. "Were you baptized into the name of Paul?"	A believer's allegiance can *only* be to Christ.

Split churches today cannot improve upon this strategy. Healing and unity are found in Jesus Christ—in realizing both who He is and what He has done for us and will do for us if we will allow Him.

These three questions together form a collective affirmation: The person who responds in faith to Christ must give himself or herself totally to Christ.

THE PRIORITY OF PREACHING (vv. 14–17)

Paul next emphasized the fact that he had baptized few of his converts. This ministry he entrusted to others, while he devoted his primary energies to preaching the gospel. Paul expressed this concern lest converts exaggerate the importance of the role of the baptizer (v. 15). He was equally concerned that no one exaggerate the skills one uses to proclaim the gospel. Actions that draw attention to the one proclaiming the message shift the focus from the message to the messenger. When this happens, the cross of Christ is "emptied of its power" (v. 17).

■ *Paul's first major topic was the problem of*
■ *factions in the Corinthian church. Some*
■ *were claiming to follow Paul, some Apollos,*
■ *others Cephas, and yet others Christ. Paul*
■ *showed the sinfulness and folly of such divi-*
■ *sion. God does not act in the way human wis-*
■ *dom might expect. God redeems men and*
■ *women by the foolishness of the cross, not by*
■ *anything that would enhance human pride.*
■ *Paul taught that the gospel message did not*
■ *originate in profound human thought but in*
■ *the Holy Spirit Himself.*

THE MESSAGE OF THE CROSS (1:18–31)

The emphasis on the priority of preaching in verse 17 now advances to a focus on the message of the cross. It is certainly one of the greatest passages in the New Testament. At this point in his letter, Paul shifted to the message of the Cross because the Corinthian church showed a great misunderstanding of the essential truth of the gospel:

- they had a wrong concept of wisdom (1:18–2:5);
- they had a wrong concept of the gospel (2:6–13); and

"Perishing"

This word is a compound made up of the preposition "out of" and the verb "to destroy." It means "to ruin," "to be lost," "to lose utterly." "The preposition in the compound is perfective and the present tense indicates that the goal is ideally reached. A complete transformation of the subjects is required to bring them out of the ruin implicit in their state" (Fritz Rienecker, *Linguistic Key to the Greek New Testament* [Grand Rapids: Zondervan, 1980], 387).

• they had a wrong concept of spirituality (2:14–3:4).

In verses 18–31, Paul addressed the Corinthians' wrong concept of wisdom and set forth three distinct truths about the cross of Christ:

1. The cross of Christ is necessary to the knowledge of God (vv. 18–21).
2. The cross of Christ requires the response of faith (vv. 22–25).
3. The cross of Christ allows for no boasting in God's presence (vv. 26–31).

Necessary to the Knowledge of God (vv. 18–21)
God seeks to make Himself known to us, and He uses many media to confront us. These include nature, conscience, the Scriptures, and His self-disclosure in the cross of Jesus Christ.

However, the world neither appreciates nor understands God's confrontations. The message of the cross is "foolishness to those who are perishing" (v. 18). The world has its own spokespersons: the wise man, the professional scholar, and the subtle debater (v. 20). It has it own criteria for acceptance or rejection, which is visible evidence or rational proofs. And it has its own prevailing attitude: self-sufficiency and confidence in the power of its own reasoning and technology.

God's Revelation to Us

MEDIA	PASSAGE
Nature	Rom. 1:20
Conscience	Rom. 2:14–16
Scriptures	Rom. 3:1, 2
Cross of Jesus Christ	1 Cor. 1:18–21

In verse 21 Paul rendered the startling indictment of human wisdom: "The world through its wisdom did not know him." The fatal flaw in man's wisdom and ingenuity is that it leaves him without the knowledge of God.

Paul went on to write that "God was pleased through the foolishness of what was preached to save those who believe" (v. 21). "What was preached" refers not to the act of preaching, but to the content of the proclamation.

Requires the Response of Faith (vv. 22–25)

In verses 22–25, Paul mentioned two groups for whom the call to faith in a crucified Lord was especially offensive. These groups were:

The Jews. The Jews looked for signs that identify the Messiah, who would be their deliverer from Roman oppression. Because there was no place for a Messiah who would die on the cross, faith in Christ was a stumbling block to the Jew.

The Greeks. The Greeks embraced human wisdom and demanded rational, empirical proofs. That an itinerant Jewish teacher sentenced to die on the cross was the Son of God and Savior of the world seemed foolish.

Verse 25 affirmed to Paul's readers that all who respond in faith to God's call in Jesus Christ experience Him as God's power and wisdom, whether Jews or Greeks.

Allows No Boasting in God's Presence (vv. 26–31)

Paul reminded the Corinthians of who they were and where they came from. Not many were rich, famous, and powerful. He then said something startling. God delights in taking those whom the world despises and raising them up. In this way, it becomes clear to all that what has been done is God's work.

Paul closed this chapter with the exclamation, "Let him who boasts boast in the Lord" (v. 31).

- *Paul shifted to the message of the cross*
- *because the Corinthian church showed a great*
- *misunderstanding of the essential truth of the*
- *gospel. He addressed the Corinthians' wrong*
- *concept of wisdom and set forth three distinct*
- *truths about the cross of Christ: (1) the cross*
- *of Christ is necessary to the knowledge of*
- *God; (2) the cross of Christ requires the*
- *response of faith; and (3) the cross of Christ*
- *allows for no boasting in God's presence.*

QUESTIONS TO GUIDE YOUR STUDY

1. Paul opened this letter with an expanded salutation. From this salutation, what do we learn about the church?
2. Why was Paul thankful for the Corinthian believers? What was his prayer for them?
3. What kind of report had Paul received about the Corinthian church? What was Paul's response to the troubles at Corinth?
4. Describe the message of the cross. What are its essential truths?

This chapter continues Paul's theme of the gospel and the wisdom of the world. Some of the Corinthian believers were enamored with the wisdom of certain men. They thought the church could benefit more from the world's wisdom and philosophy to win converts to Christ rather than relying on the message of the Cross.

PAUL'S MINISTRY IN CORINTH (2:1–5)

Paul reminded the Corinthians about the message he brought, the manner in which he brought it, and the motivation that impelled him when he came to Corinth. Recall that Paul affirmed both the speech and wisdom of the Corinthians as he opened his letter. Now he told them that in his communicating the gospel to them, he relied neither on impressive speech nor wisdom.

His Message (vv. 1, 2)

Paul was single-minded. He intentionally focused on one truth: Jesus Christ and Him crucified. With his rich background, he could have imparted many things to the Corinthians. But he chose to focus on the most important.

His Manner (vv. 1, 3, 4)

Evidently Paul was not in his top form when he came to Corinth. He was suffering emotionally and physically, and he came across as weak. Consequently, Paul relied not on his own power but the power of the Holy Spirit as he presented Christ.

Paul was one of the best educated men of his day. He was thoroughly trained as a Jewish rabbi. But his learning likely went beyond his own religious tradition. His early years were spent in Tarsus—home of a major university. We don't know whether he studied at that university, but growing up in Tarsus prepared Paul to be at home in a variety of worlds. It's evident that he was skilled in numerous languages. Paul was a Roman citizen—an indication that he was born into a family cosmopolitan in outlook.

Believers and churches today are seeking to meet the challenges of an increasingly urbanized society that depends on advancing, new technologies. But they cannot improve upon the essential strategy Paul reveals here. Today's churches often fail to gain New Testament results because they do not rely on the power of the Holy Spirit to take the message and make it effective in the lives of hearers.

His Motivation (v. 5).

Paul's compelling desire was for other people to place their faith in the power of God rather than in the wisdom of men.

■ *Paul preached the gospel to Corinth, a great*
■ *urban center of his day. His basic message*
■ *was simple and clear: "Jesus Christ and him*
■ *crucified." Throughout his ministry Paul*
■ *understood his responsibility as a messenger*
■ *of God and depended upon God's power, not*
■ *his own strength, to carry out his mission.*

CHRISTIAN WISDOM (2:6–16)

To guard against his repudiation of worldly wisdom being interpreted as hostility toward all wisdom, Paul gave his readers a concept of wisdom that is distinctly Christian.

The Gospel Is Distinct from Human Wisdom (vv. 6–9)

The word *however* introduces a contrast between the world's wisdom and the Christian wisdom of which Paul spoke.Throughout this section of the chapter (vv. 6–16), Paul built his view of Christian wisdom, as the chart on page 19 shows.

The Role of the Spirit (vv. 10–13)

The divine origin of the message is the Holy Spirit. Paul revealed at least two of the Spirit's activities with regard to His role of revealing the wisdom of God.

"The Spirit searches all things" (v. 10). The phrase "searches all things" means that the Spirit penetrates all things, even the "deep things of God." The word *deep* often refers to the unfathomable depths of the sea.

Paul's View on Christian Wisdom

KEY POINT	PASSAGE
1. Christian wisdom exists among mature believers.	v. 6
2. Christian wisdom is not to be confused with the world's wisdom.	vv. 6, 8
3. Christian wisdom centers on God's redemptive plan through the ages.	vv. 7, 9
4. Christian wisdom is revealed to us by the Spirit.	vv. 10–12
5. Christian wisdom is imparted to others by us who have been taught by the Spirit.	v. 13
6. Christian wisdom is folly to the unspiritual person.	vv. 14–16

The Spirit "knows the thoughts of God" (v. 11). Paul presented the argument that nobody really knows what goes on inside a person's mind—the memories, reflections, motives—except for that person's spirit. In a similar way, no one can know what goes on in God's mind, except the Spirit of God.

In verse 12, we come to the central issue of verses 6–16: When we come to Christ, we receive God's Spirit, who searches and knows the mind of God. He is able to impart the things of God to us. Worldly wisdom, however impressive, cannot begin to do for us what God's Spirit can.

Spiritual Discernment (vv. 14–16)
Paul contrasted the unspiritual person's inability to make right judgments with that of the spiritual person.

Borrowing from Isa. 64:4, Paul quoted, "No eye has seen, no ear has heard, no mind has conceived what God has prepared for those who love him" (1 Cor. 2:9). He appears to be making two points here:

1. God's ways are not conceivable by the human mind.

2. The human mind is ignorant of the salvation God has prepared for those who love Him.

Therefore, our human methods of comprehension—"eyes," "ears," understanding—cannot give us any idea of the wonderful things God has already prepared for "those who love him."

Characteristics of the Unspiritual Person

CHARACTERISTIC	REASON
Does not accept the things that come from the Spirit	They are foolishness
Cannot understand the things that come from the Spirit	They are spiritually discerned

- *To guard against his repudiation of worldly*
- *wisdom being interpreted as discrediting all*
- *wisdom, Paul gave his readers a distinctly*
- *Christian concept of wisdom. Christian wis-*
- *dom exists among mature believers, and it is*
- *the Holy Spirit who reveals the wisdom of*
- *God to believers, for only the Spirit knows*
- *the mind of God.*

QUESTIONS TO GUIDE YOUR STUDY

1. What characterized Paul's ministry at Corinth? What can we learn from his strategy that can be applied today?
2. What is the difference between worldly wisdom and Christian wisdom?
3. What is the role of the Spirit in revealing the wisdom of God?
4. What is spiritual discernment? How does it work in the believer?

1 CORINTHIANS 3

In this chapter Paul took a more direct approach with his indictment of the divisions in the church at Corinth. Using metaphors from agriculture, architecture, and Judaism, Paul delivered insight and warnings that define the proper roles of faithful servants. Key points of this chapter include:

1. Although many laborers contribute to the "planting" and "watering" of the seed of the gospel, only God gives that seed growth.
2. As Christians labor in doing the work of God's kingdom, only genuine building materials will stand the test of judgment.
3. Believers are God's temple because God's Spirit dwells within them. They are not to destroy God's temple, or God will destroy them.
4. Believers are to draw a distinction between worldly wisdom and God's wisdom, and not be deceived by the world's way of thinking.

"WORLDLY" CHURCH MEMBERS (3:1–4)

Paul lamented that he could not address his readers as spiritual people (v. 1). Instead, he must address them as "worldly," because of the jealousy and strife in their midst (v. 3). As "mere infants in Christ," they still required a milk diet. Therefore, Paul could not set before them "solid food" to digest.

These first four verses set the stage for the rest of the chapter in which Paul dealt with the division within the church. What follows is vintage Paul—a powerful mixture of insight, warning, and appeal. He delivered three powerful metaphors regarding the work of the servant.

Metaphors of the Laborer

METAPHOR	OBJECT	REASON FOR USE	KEY POINT
Agriculture (vv. 5–9)	Field	Insight	Only God gives growth
Architecture (vv. 10–15)	Building	Warning	Only genuine building materials withstand the test
Judaism (vv. 16, 17)	Temple	Strong warning	Believers are God's temple, and God's temple is sacred

■ *Paul viewed the Corinthian believers as mere*
■ *infants in Christ. Because of their jealousy*
■ *and strife, they were not mature enough for*
■ *the "solid food" he had hoped to give them.*

GOD GIVES THE GROWTH (3:5–9)

Paul used two key terms that require special attention from the reader: "servants" and "Lord." God's servants are many, but God alone is Lord. The roles of the two must never be confused. However, the Corinthians obviously were giving to certain servants of God their devotion that rightly belonged only to God.

This metaphor provides an encouraging truth for all Christians of all ages. It teaches that every believer has equal access to God's favor. Arduous labor is possible for all God's servants, whereas a large harvest is not always.

To clarify the roles of the servant and the Lord, Paul used an agricultural metaphor to portray the important but subordinate role of man in the work of the gospel. In reality, Paul had "planted" the gospel at Corinth, while Apollos, who came later, "watered" it. As a result of the faithfulness of both these men, many were saved. But what was the proper explanation of this harvest? Did Paul or Apollos accomplish their salvation? The answer is no! It is *God* who gives the growth. Only He has the power to cause the seed of the gospel message to grow.

An Agricultural Lesson

ANALOGY	EXPLANATION	AGENT	RESULTS
Field (v. 9)	The church at Corinth		A harvest
Planting (v. 6)	Spreading the seed of the gospel message	Christian laborers	Laborer rewarded for labor
Watering (v. 6)	Nurturing and cultivating the implanted seed	Christian laborers	Laborer rewarded for labor
Growth (v. 7)	Development and fruitfulness of the seed	God	God's blessings on the work of His laborers

Apollos

Apollos was an Alexandrian Jew who came to Ephesus following Paul's first visit and was taught Christian doctrine by Priscilla and Aquila. Apollos was skilled in interpreting Scripture, and there is evidence that he was a more polished speaker than Paul or Peter. Although one of the splinter groups in Corinth seemed to pit Apollos against Paul, there is no indication that Apollos encouraged this. In 1 Corinthians 16:12 Paul referred to Apollos as "our brother." In one of Paul's latest letters, Titus, Paul urged Titus to help Apollos on his way.

■ *To clarify the roles of the servant and the*
■ *Lord, Paul used an agricultural metaphor to*
■ *portray the important but subordinate role of*
■ *humankind in the work of the gospel. Both*
■ *"planting" and "watering" by the servants*
■ *are required for an abundant harvest of the*
■ *gospel message. But growth comes from God.*
■ *Only He has the power to cause the seed of*
■ *the gospel message to grow.*

TEST OF FIRE (3:10–15)

Paul now employed an architectural metaphor. In this metaphor, Christ is the only foundation that could be laid. Paul had already laid this

"Gold, silver, precious stones"

"The durable materials are three (gold, silver, marble or precious stone), perishable materials (pieces of wood, hay, stubble), of a palace on one hand, of a mud hut on the other, (Lightfoot). Gold was freely used by the ancients in their palaces. Their marble and granite pillars are still the wonder and despair of modern man. The wooden huts had hay and stubble which were used to hold the wood pieces together and to thatch the roof. It is not clear whether Paul's metaphor refers to the persons as in God's building in verse 9 or to the character of the teaching as in verse 13. Probably both ideas are involved, considering the penalty for shoddy work (v. 15) and shoddy men (v. 17). The teaching may not always be vicious and harmful. It may only be indifferent and worthless. A co-worker with God in this great temple should put in his very best effort" (A. T. Robertson, *Word Pictures in the New Testament*, "Epistles of Paul," vol. 4, 97).

foundation through his ministry of spreading the gospel message in Corinth. Now others were building on that foundation, and they needed to take care how they were doing it.

The adequacy or integrity of any building material is shown when it is subjected to a test. The Christian's work will be tested by fire on the day of judgment, showing it for what it is (v. 13).

The believer whose building materials are combustible, including wood, hay, or straw, will find his or her work consumed with fire—"burned up." This word refers to something that is burned up *completely*. Those who use noncombustible building materials such as gold, silver, or costly stones (granite and marble) will find their labor will stand the test. Such a laborer will "receive a reward." Those who have built poorly will suffer loss, but they themselves will be saved as a person who is rescued from a fire.

Paul intended that his reminder of God's impending judgment upon the work of all His servants should give pause to those in Corinth who were responsible for divisions in the church.

■ *Paul used an architectural metaphor to drive*
■ *home a point about the importance of the genu-*
■ *ineness of one's building materials for the work*
■ *of the kingdom. The adequacy or integrity of*
■ *any building material depends upon the test it*
■ *will have to meet. That test for the Christian's*
■ *building is fire on the day of judgment.*

DESTROYING GOD'S TEMPLE (3:16, 17)

Paul used yet another metaphor—a temple. This metaphor applies to all believers, anytime and anywhere. The temple does not refer to the structure in which believers meet to worship. Rather, Christians themselves *are* the temple of God. They are His temple because God's Spirit dwells within them. Paul's original readers, those responsible for the divisions in the church at Corinth, had lost sight of this basic truth and needed correction. Nothing destroys a church more completely than dissension and strife.

Because of this, Paul issued this strong warning that God will destroy those who destroy His temple (vv. 16, 17).

- Paul used the metaphor of a temple to illustrate the destructive nature of dissension and strife that existed in the Corinthian church.
- Because the Holy Spirit indwells believers, they are the temple of God and must not allow such destructive forces to control them.
- Paul issued his strongest warning yet: "If anyone destroys God's temple, God will destroy that person."

FOLLY OF WORLDLY WISDOM (3:18–23)

The Believer Is to Avoid Self-Deception (v. 18)

In this final portion of chapter 3, Paul drew a sharp distinction between worldly wisdom and God's wisdom. Paul exhorted his readers, "Do not deceive yourselves" (v. 18).

The Craftiness of the Worldly Wise (vv. 19, 20)

God sees through the pretensions of human wisdom. Paul quoted two passages from the Old Testament to illustrate this truth.

"Deceive"

This is a powerful word in the Greek text of the New Testament. It is a compound word made up of the prefixed preposition "out of" and the verb "to deceive." The preposition serves to intensify the action of the verb. This word means "to deceive thoroughly or wholly." To appeal to the will of his readers, Paul made this word a command. Paul applied this word to self-deception. Those who destroy rather than build the church are deceiving themselves, for judgment awaits them.

Paul supported his indictment of worldly wisdom by citing two passages from the Old Testament: (1) "He catches the wise in their craftiness" (Job 5:13); and (2) "The LORD knows the thoughts of man; he knows they are futile" (Ps. 94:11).

No More Boasting (vv. 21–23)

In these verses Paul sought to reverse the partisan cries of the Corinthian believers. They had been boasting of their loyalties to their favorite leaders (Paul, Apollos, Cephas). These loyalties divided the church into rival factions. Paul reminded them that they all belonged to Christ.

■ *Paul drew a sharp distinction between*
■ *worldly wisdom and God's wisdom, and he*
■ *exhorted his readers, "Do not deceive your-*
■ *selves." God views the wisdom of this world*
■ *as foolishness. Believers are not to embrace*
■ *such wisdom, but rather to embrace the*
■ *inheritance that is theirs in Jesus Christ.*

QUESTIONS TO GUIDE YOUR STUDY

1. Paul used an agricultural metaphor to illustrate the work of the gospel. What is Paul teaching with this metaphor?
2. What is the point of Paul's architectural metaphor?
3. What is the point of Paul's metaphor of the temple?
4. In his teaching on the folly of wisdom, Paul instructed believers not to deceive themselves. What does it mean to deceive oneself? Are there consequences for doing so?

Paul's warnings in the previous chapter do not imply that human leaders are unimportant. He was very clear that people are saved only by Jesus Christ, and there is no other basis for salvation. Church leaders build on this foundation. From this thought, Paul appealed to the Corinthians to act on what he had written them. Paul's key points in this chapter include:

1. The responsibility of church leaders and the importance of their example to other believers.
2. The "secret things of God" granted to leaders are things that human wisdom cannot discover but can only be revealed by God.

THE SERVANT'S ROLE (4:1–7)

Paul addressed a church that was divided into partisan groups that were boasting about their identity with one leader as over against another. Paul countered this misplaced devotion by instructing the Corinthians to consider their leaders as "entrusted with the secret things of God" (v. 1). "Those entrusted" are *stewards*.

The primary qualification of stewards is that they be found trustworthy. Because they deal with what belongs to another, they must have their master's interests at heart and avoid any kind of self-serving.

Paul had apparently been evaluated by some of the Corinthians. Perhaps he had even been compared to Peter and Apollos. Paul didn't put a lot of weight on this evaluation or any other human evaluation—including his evaluation of himself. What mattered was God's appraisal of him.

A steward was the "manager of a household, which often was a trusted slave put in charge of the whole household. The word emphasizes that one is entrusted with great responsibility and accountability" (Fritz Rienecker, *Linguistic Key to the Greek New Testament* [Grand Rapids: Zondervan, 1980], 395). In this passage, Paul referred to leaders who are stewards and what has been entrusted, or what they are to administer.

He urged the Corinthians to be patient and await the judgment that would take place at Christ's second coming. At that time, the hearts of all people would be laid bare before the One who even now reads the thoughts, desires, and motives of each person. At that time, God would give appropriate praise to His servant.

The purpose of Paul's referring to Apollos and himself in verses 6, 7 was to keep the Corinthians from taking "pride in one man over against another" (v. 6). Both Paul and Apollos were servants of Christ, not rival leaders.

■ *Paul addressed a group of believers who*
■ *were divided into partisan groups that were*
■ *boasting about their identity with one leader*
■ *as over against another. Paul countered this*
■ *misplaced devotion by instructing the Corin-*
■ *thians to consider their leaders as stewards*
■ *who are "entrusted with the secret things of*
■ *God." The primary qualification of stewards*
■ *is that they be persons who are worthy of*
■ *trust. Both Paul and Apollos were faithful*
■ *servants of Christ, not rivals.*

DEFLATION BY SATIRE (4:8–13)

Contrasts (vv. 8–11)

By favoring one leader over another, the Corinthians were judging the merits of the apostles. There was an implied claim of superiority in what they were doing. Paul sought to deflate their pride. In a series of exclamations, some of which echo themes he had touched on earlier in his letter, Paul contrasted their imagined estate with the actual lot of the apostles, whom the

Corinthians were presuming to judge. The following chart organizes these exclamations.

Paul's Contrast Between the Corinthians and the Apostles

THE CORINTHIANS	THE APOSTLES	CROSS-REFERENCE
1. "Already you have all you want! Already you have become rich! You have become kings—and that without us!" (v. 8).	1. "God has put us apostles on display at the end of the procession, like men condemned to die!" (v. 9).	1:18–25; 3:18, 19
2. "You are so wise in Christ!" (v. 10).	2. "We are fools for Christ" (v. 10).	1:18–25; 2:3–5
3. "You are strong" (v. 10).	3. "We are weak." (v. 10).	
4. "You are honored" (v. 10).	4. "We are dishonored!" (v. 10).	

Three Antitheses (vv. 12, 13a)

In verses 12, 13a, Paul delivered three antitheses that do more than state the apostles' hardships and their responses to improper treatment. They are clear reflections of the teachings of Jesus and are the responses of one who imitates Christ:

- "when we are cursed, we bless";
- "when we are persecuted, we endure it"; and
- "when we are slandered, we answer kindly."

A Final Metaphor of Humiliation (v. 13)

To accent the world's feeling toward the apostles, Paul used a very graphic and unflattering description of him and his fellow apostles: "We

"Refuse"

This word is a compound made up of the preposition "around" and the verb "to wipe." It refers to that which is removed by the process of cleaning dirt off, scouring, scum. Whereas the word *scum* indicates a rinsing, this word indicates a "scrapping" of a dirty vessel. It was used in the papyri in a letter greeting conveying the idea of "your humble and devoted servant." (Taken from *Vine's Complete Expository Dictionary of Old and New Testament Words* [Nashville: Thomas Nelson, 1996].)

have become the scum of the earth, the refuse of the world" (v. 13).

■ *By favoring one leader over another, the*
■ *Corinthians were judging the merits of the*
■ *apostles. Seeking to deflate their pride, Paul*
■ *provided a series of exclamations that con-*
■ *trasted the Corinthians' imagined estate with*
■ *the actual lot of the apostles, whom the*
■ *Corinthians were presuming to judge. Paul*
■ *closed this portion of his letter by embracing*
■ *responses that are indicative of a person who*
■ *is imitating Christ.*

PAUL'S PERSONAL APPEAL (4:14–21)

In verses 14, 15, Paul assumed the role of a father counseling his children: "In Christ Jesus I became your father through the gospel" (v. 15). He was clear that his hard words were not to shame them, but to warn so that they might do what is right. He encouraged the Corinthians to become imitators of him and announced that he was sending Timothy to minister to them for that reason. He also mentioned that he himself would be visiting them soon (v. 19).

In the next verses, Paul pointed out that some of the Corinthian believers had become "arrogant." He urged the Corinthians to undergo a behavioral change or they would be subject to Paul's discipline: "Shall I come to you with a whip, or in love and with a gentle spirit?" (v. 21). He placed the issue before them and left the choice to them.

■ Paul assumed the role of a father counseling
■ his children, and encouraged the Corinthians
■ to become imitators of him. He also urged the
■ Corinthians to undergo a behavior change or
■ be subject to his discipline.

QUESTIONS TO GUIDE YOUR STUDY

1. Paul explained the responsibility of church leaders and said that they are really "stewards." What is a steward, and what does a steward do?

2. In verses 8–13, what is the point of Paul's several exclamations?

3. How did the world perceive the apostles and their work, according to Paul?

4. How did Paul couch his personal appeal to the Corinthians? What was the content of his appeal?

As in any day, the pressures to conform to an immoral society were strong in the church at Corinth. In chapter 5, Paul responded to reports that had reached him about an incident of incest involving a member of the congregation. In this chapter, he rebuked the church for tolerating such flagrant immorality in its midst and demanded that they exclude the member from the congregation.

"Sexual immorality"

"Sexual immorality" translates the Greek word *porneia*. It is used of illicit sexual intercourse and "refers to general sexual acts outside of legal marriage" (Fritz Rienecker, *Linguistic Key to the Greek New Testament* [Grand Rapids: Zondervan, 1980], 399). The Greeks used a different word for the act of adultery: "*moicheia* is technically adultery on the part of the married (Mark 7:21)" (A. T. Robertson, *Word Pictures in the New Testament*, "Epistles of Paul," vol. 4, 111).

SHOCKING PERMISSIVENESS IN THE CORINTHIAN CHURCH (5:1, 2)

Paul had heard reports of sexual immorality among the Corinthians. The problem involved a man in the church who was living in an illicit sexual relationship with his stepmother (the probable meaning of the phrase "his father's wife"). She was probably a pagan, for Paul did not include her in his instructions.

The incident was especially shameful because the father and son had engaged in sexual relationships with the same woman. The Old Testament Scriptures strictly forbade such behavior (Lev. 18:7, 8; 20:11). Even the Romans prohibited such unions. But the church's attitude toward the evil taking place within their congregation was one of pride and arrogance.

The Corinthians were so busy priding themselves on their spirituality that they were ignoring the immoral behavior of the member. At stake was the integrity of the Christian witness to an immoral society, but the proud Corinthian believers were too unspiritual to recognize the severity of the problem. Paul rebuked them for their failure to respond properly to the offending member (v. 2). "You are proud!" (v. 2), Paul declared.

■ *Paul drew his readers' attention to a case of*
■ *incest at Corinth. Although the Christian wit-*
■ *ness to an immoral society was at stake, the*
■ *proud Corinthian believers were too unspiri-*
■ *tual to recognize the severity and deal with*
■ *the problem.*

EXCLUSION OF THE OFFENDER DEMANDED (5:3–5)

Although he was not present with the Corinthian believers, Paul took responsibility for correcting the state of affairs that existed in the congregation. He passed judgment on the member who was guilty of immoral conduct and instructed the entire fellowship to deal with the problem.

The congregation was to meet on the issue. After they gathered in the name of Jesus Christ and with His power, Paul ordered that they "hand this man over to Satan, so that the sinful nature may be destroyed and his spirit saved on the day of the Lord" (v. 5). We can make at least three observations from Paul's handling of this incident of immorality in the Corinthian church:

1. The form of discipline applied here was exclusion from the church, which was suggested in verse 2.
2. Apparently the world outside the church was regarded as Satan's domain.
3. The purpose of the actions was redemptive, not merely punitive.

■ *Paul took responsibility for correcting the*
■ *problem that existed in the congregation. He*
■ *passed judgment on a member who was guilty*
■ *of immoral conduct and instructed the entire*
■ *fellowship to deal with the problem by exclud-*
■ *ing the offending member from the church.*

Leaven in the Bible

Leaven was a small portion of fermented dough used to ferment other dough. It often symbolized corruptive influence. *Unleavened* bread was required for the Feast of Unleavened Bread, which was celebrated in conjunction with the Passover festival (Lev. 23:4–8). It reminded the Israelites of their hasty departure from Egypt and warned them against corruptive influences.

EVIL AS LEAVEN (5:6–8)

Paul criticized the Corinthians for boasting. They prided themselves on being an exemplary congregation but condoned sin in their midst. He used the illustration of leaven to show them how dangerous their attitude was.

Several Old Testament passages shed light on the observance of Passover and the Feast of Unleavened Bread. These passages include Exod. 12:1–51; Lev. 23:4–6; and Deut. 16:1–8. An understanding of those Old Testament Scriptures provide an appreciation for Paul's messages in verses 6–8.

Paul rebuked the Corinthians for their complacency regarding the immoral member. He likened the presence of this person in the church to old leaven that would contaminate the whole batch (v. 6). Paul called for a cleansing of the old leaven. Christ, our "Passover lamb," has been sacrificed, and the call given to celebrate the festival with "bread of sincerity and truth" (v. 7).

Paul presented his readers with a principle of New Testament church discipline. When a congregation, or the church at large, condones immorality, the moral fiber of the church is weakened. None escape its contamination. The *whole* lump is affected. No church or fellowship may celebrate deliverance from sin while sheltering sin among its members.

■ *The Corinthians prided themselves on being*
■ *an exemplary congregation but condoned sin*
■ *in their midst. Paul used the illustration of*
■ *leaven to show them how dangerous their*
■ *attitude was. When believers condone immo-*
■ *rality among themselves, the moral fiber of*
■ *the entire church is weakened.*

PREVIOUS LETTER CLARIFIED (5:9–13)

At this point in his letter, Paul found it necessary to clear up a misunderstanding that occurred as a result of a letter he had sent earlier to Corinth. He had urged his readers not to continue in fellowship with immoral church members. The

Corinthians, however, had understood Paul to mean that they must withdraw from associations with all immoral persons in the world (v. 10). Paul corrected this misunderstanding, indicating that it is God's responsibility to judge those outside the church (v. 13).

The problem with the church at Corinth was not that they were living in the midst of an immoral society. Rather, it was their low estimate of what it means be the people of God in such a setting. They had permitted the immoral society around them to invade their midst. For the fourth time in this chapter, Paul demanded that the congregation exclude the immoral church member from the fellowship.

- *Paul found it necessary to clear up a misunder-*
- *standing that occurred as a result of a letter he*
- *had sent earlier to Corinth. He had urged his*
- *readers not to continue in fellowship with*
- *immoral church members, reminding them*
- *that God will judge those outside their church.*

QUESTIONS TO GUIDE YOUR STUDY

1. What prompted Paul's rebuke of the Corinthian believers in verses 1, 2?

2. In Paul's instructions for dealing with members guilty of immoral conduct, what do we learn about church discipline?

3. What is the lesson of *leaven* Paul is teaching here?

4. Paul cleared up a misunderstanding from a previous letter to the Corinthians. What was this misunderstanding, and what was Paul's counsel to them?

In this chapter, Paul chastised the Corinthians for their factious spirit. Their active part in lawsuits before heathen judges was evidence of their unspiritual attitudes. Paul provided instructions on dealing with disputes within the Christian community. He then went on to discuss the kind of conduct that excludes people from the kingdom of God.

THE PROBLEM (6:1–4)

Paul turned his attention to personal disputes among the church members. Evidently, some members of the congregation were contending about personal rights or business matters. Unable to resolve these differences, they were appealing to courts of law.

In these opening verses of the chapter, Paul presented two main points for his readers:

Paul was not depreciating courts or implying that all pagan judges are corrupt and incapable of administering justice. His concern, instead, was that the Corinthians were depreciating the gospel by their readiness to sue one another.

1. He considered it ludicrous for those destined to participate in the final judgment to show themselves "not competent to judge trivial cases" (v. 2). Those who are to deal with the issues of the ages ought to be able to deal with the problems of the moment.
2. He considered it tragic for believers to carry their disputes before pagan judges. To do so was to discredit the gospel in the eyes of the pagan society to which they were to bear witness.

■ *Members of the congregation were contend-*
■ *ing about personal rights or business mat-*
■ *ters. Unable to resolve these differences, they*
■ *were appealing to courts of law. Paul pro-*
■ *vides instructions for keeping the resolution*
■ *of disputes among believers rather than tak-*
■ *ing them before pagan judges, where the wit-*
■ *ness of the gospel could be discredited.*

ALTERNATIVES TO LITIGATION (6:5–8)

Arbitration Within the Church (vv. 5–6)

The Corinthian believers boasted of their wisdom. Paul asked them why it was necessary for them to go outside their congregation to find a person competent to render a judgment in their disputes.

With arbitration within the Corinthian congregation an option, Paul was distressed that "one brother goes to law against another—and this in front of unbelievers" (v. 6).

Enduring the Wrong (vv. 7, 8)

That serious disputes and breakdowns in relationships existed among the Corinthians was an indication that they "have been completely defeated already" (v. 7).

Rather than discrediting the gospel by dragging disputes into the pagan courts, Paul advised the Corinthians to endure the wrong done to them: "Why not rather be wronged?" Apparently some of the Corinthians were suing others in the courts attempting to defraud one another (v. 8).

Under Roman rule, the Jews enjoyed a large measure of autonomy. Disputes among those in the Jewish community were settled among themselves. Indeed, the rabbis taught that it was unlawful for a Jew to seek a judge's decision in pagan courts. Even within the pagan world, there were religious brotherhoods and mutual-benefit societies that pledged not to sue one another in the courts. Disputes among these groups were settled through arbitration among themselves.

- *Because the Corinthians boasted of their*
- *wisdom, Paul asked them why it was neces-*
- *sary for them to go outside their congrega-*
- *tion to settle their disputes. They were to*
- *settle their disputes by arbitration within the*
- *Corinthian congregation, rather than dis-*
- *credit the gospel by dragging disputes into*
- *the pagan courts.*

RELATION TO THE KINGDOM OF GOD (6:9–11)

In verses 1–8 Paul focused on a particular form of unrighteous conduct—the readiness to sue or defraud one another in court. He now broadened his discussion to include other forms of unrighteousness.

Warning to the Wicked (vv. 9, 10)

Paul warned the Corinthians not to be deceived. Literally, he was telling his readers, "Do not continue to be deceived."

Twice he affirmed that the unrighteous have no inheritance in God's kingdom (v. 9). He repeated this warning in verse 10, where he listed several acts of unrighteousness that were characteristic of the wicked. Six of these are a repeat of what Paul listed in 5:10, 11, with four additions. The following chart lists these and their meanings.

Sins of the Wicked

SIN	MEANING
Sexual immorality	Unlawful sexual activity with the spouse of another person
Idolatry	Worshiping and serving of idols
Adultery	Indulgence in fornication
Male prostitution	Technical term for a passive partner in homosexual relations
Homosexuality	Homosexual activities between males
Thievery	Use of force or violence in stealing
Greediness	Desire of having more and seeking fulfillment by any means
Drunkenness	State of intoxication
Slander	Use of abusive language
Swindling	Act of extortion

The Basis of the Believer's Righteousness (v. 11)
Paul told the Corinthians that, as believers in Christ, they were no longer to be among those who commit such acts of unrighteousness. He now provided three metaphors that form the basis of his premise: "You were washed, you were sanctified, you were justified in the name of the Lord Jesus Christ and by the Spirit of our God" (v. 11).

The Believer's Basis for Righteous Living

WORK OF SALVATION	SIGNIFICANCE TO BELIEVERS
"Washed"	They are washed from the filth of their former lifestyles.
"Sanctified"	They are set apart for holy, godly living that contrasts their former wickedness.
"Justified"	Because of their justification, they may inherit the kingdom of God.

"Washed"

This word is a compound in the Greek language, and is made up of the preposition "away, off" and the verb "to wash." It means "to wash off something." The preposition has a "perfective" force, which means that it emphasizes the completeness of the action of the verb "to wash." With this word Paul told his readers at Corinth that they had been completely washed of their former filthy and wicked lifestyles.

■ *Paul broadened his discussion to include other*
■ *forms of unrighteousness. After commanding*
■ *readers, "Do not continue to be deceived," he*
■ *listed several acts of unrighteousness that*
■ *paint the character of the wicked. The Corin-*
■ *thians, however, were not to be among those*
■ *who commit such acts of unrighteousness, for*
■ *they had been washed, sanctified, and justified*
■ *"in the name of the Lord Jesus Christ and by*
■ *the Spirit of our God."*

SEXUAL IMMORALITY (6:12–20)

Paul's discussion of sexual immorality is the most extensive on this subject in all his letters. He challenged the Corinthians' casual attitude toward sexual immorality. He then made a case for sexual purity.

Refuting Popular Slogans (vv. 12–14)

As we do today, the Corinthians used popular slogans, or catch-phrases. Paul quoted two of these that some of the church members may have been using to rationalize their attitude regarding sexual indulgence. He used these quotes as points of departure for setting forth a Christian view of sexual behavior.

"Everything is permissible for me" (v. 12). Paul added a qualifier to this slogan that related it to Christian freedom: "But not everything is beneficial." Paul insisted that the Christian exercise freedom in a thoroughly responsible way. Otherwise, the believer's freedom becomes license. And license leads to slavery.

"Food for the stomach and the stomach for food" (v. 13). Here Paul confronted those who excused their sexual sins by declaring that the

body had no significance. He tied the importance of the body to the coming resurrection (v. 14).

The significance of Paul's refuting these slogans is that in both cases the Corinthians were rationalizing sexual immorality as allowable or irrelevant.

Intercourse with Prostitutes (vv. 15–17)

For the citizens of Corinth, sexual relations with cult prostitutes carried a religious significance. It signified consecration to the cult goddess. For visitors to the city, such as sailors, this prostitution was nothing less than debauchery.

Paul stated that intercourse with a prostitute was a desecration of the body. He considered the believer's identification with Christ so complete that when a believer committed fornication with a prostitute, he involved Christ in the act.

Flee Sexual Immorality (vv. 18–20)

Paul followed this command to flee sexual immorality with four reasons:

1. *It has a tragic uniqueness as a sin against the body (v. 18).* No sin involves so complete a giving of the total person in a way that opposes God.

2. *It desecrates the body, which is the temple of the Holy Spirit (v. 19).* At conversion the Holy Spirit comes to dwell in the life of the believer, which makes the body of the believer a temple of the Holy Spirit. Sexual immorality profanes the Spirit's temple.

3. *It ignores the costliness of redemption (vv. 19, 20).* The Christian is not his or her own, but rather has been bought with a price—the sacrifice of Jesus Christ on the cross.

Paul commanded the Corinthians to "flee" sexual immorality (v. 18). In its grammatical context, this word meant that the fleeing was to be a continual and habitual fleeing. Because some people insist on spending time where temptation abounds, they find it difficult to resist, and then fail morally. In resisting sexual temptation, the believer does well never to underestimate its power or overestimate one's strength to refuse.

4. *It fails to glorify God in the body (v. 20).* The believer is to use his or her body to glorify God. Therefore, the body requires the highest level of Christian integrity in sexual relationships.

■ *Here Paul wrote his most extensive section*
■ *on sexual immorality. He challenged the*
■ *Corinthians' casual attitude toward the sex-*
■ *ual immorality that existed in their fellow-*
■ *ship. He closed the section with a command*
■ *to "flee" sexual immorality.*

QUESTIONS TO GUIDE YOUR STUDY

1. What problem did Paul address in 6:1–4? What was distressing him about it?
2. What was Paul's counsel for believers who had disputes with others in the congregation?
3. In 6:9, 10, Paul gave his readers a list of the sins of the wicked. Why? What is the believer's basis for righteous living?
4. Paul refuted two popular slogans of his day. What was his point?
5. What was Paul's practical counsel for avoiding sexual immorality? What reasons did he give for his counsel?

1 CORINTHIANS 7

The Corinthians had raised a series of questions for Paul. In this chapter, he responded to their concerns by addressing the issue of marriage and divorce. In this chapter Paul provided principles for marriage and gave advice to the married and the unmarried.

He moved on to offer further advice about contentment and then concluded this topic with counsel for virgins and widows.

WHERE BOTH HUSBAND AND WIFE ARE CHRISTIANS (7:1–7, 10, 11)

As the gospel was preached in Corinth, sometimes both a husband and wife became Christians. Sometimes, only one spouse became a believer, leaving a mixed marriage. Still others who responded to the gospel were unmarried or widows. The Corinthians wanted to know how becoming a Christian would affect these various relationships:

- Should a Christian continue to share life's most intimate union with a pagan partner?
- Should an unmarried Christian marry?
- Should a widowed believer remarry?
- How do these situations apply to various cultural and religious settings?

Paul answered these important questions, often deferring to the recorded teachings of Jesus. Where no recorded teachings of the Lord were available, Paul gave his own opinion "as one who by the Lord's mercy is trustworthy" (v. 25).

Paul's Preference for Celibacy (vv. 1, 2, 7)

In verse 1 Paul stated his preference for celibacy. In verse 7 he implied that his celibacy was a gift.

Some persons in Corinth may have been practicing celibacy within marriage without the consent of their spouse. This could have led to immorality on the part of the nonconsenting partner.

In this sense, his gift fit his calling. Paul did acknowledge that not all have the gift of celibacy.

A Sexual Partnership (vv. 3–6)

For marriage to provide a security against sexual temptation, both spouses must be generous with each other in the conjugal relationship. In such a relationship, "the wife's body does not belong to her alone but also to her husband. In the same way, the husband's body does not belong to him alone but also to his wife" (v. 4). Neither are to refuse sexual relations to the other except "by mutual consent and for a time" (v. 5). For such exceptional cases, Paul spelled out the details for this kind of arrangement:

- Any abstinence is to be by common consent, since the decision involves both spouses.
- It is to be for a limited time, not indefinitely.
- It is to be for a special season of prayer.

The husband and wife are to resume their normal pattern of conjugal relations "so that Satan will not tempt" them because of a lack of control.

In these opening verses of chapter 7, Paul taught some important features of the Christian concept of marriage, as the following chart details:

THE CHRISTIAN MARRIAGE

1. It is a monogamous relationship: one husband and one wife for life.

2. No premarital or extramarital sex is permitted.

3. Sex contributes to the fulfillment of the marriage relationship, and is not limited to having children.

4. The principle of mutuality prevails. The husband is to fulfill his duty to his wife and the wife to her husband.

The Sanctity of Marriage (vv. 10, 11)

A husband and wife are not to separate. Here Paul appealed to the teachings of Jesus but didn't deal with the issue of grounds for divorce. If a wife did separate from her husband, both were to remain single or be reconciled to each other.

- Paul stated his preference for celibacy. For
- married Christians, marriage is a monoga-
- mous relationship: one husband and one wife
- for life. For those who are married, to provide
- a security against sexual temptation, both
- spouses must be generous with each other.
- Neither is to refuse sexual relations to the other
- except "by mutual consent and for a time."

WHERE ONLY ONE SPOUSE IS A CHRISTIAN (7:12–24)

One question posed to Paul by the Corinthians was whether a believer ought to continue in marriage with a pagan. To this Paul gave his own opinion by emphasizing two principles: (1) the initiative belongs to the unbeliever; and (2) God calls us to live in peace.

Initiative Belongs to the Unbeliever (vv. 12–16)

Paul taught that if the unbelieving spouse desires to continue in the marriage, then the Christian partner is to comply (vv. 12, 13). If the unbelieving spouse desires to separate, the Christian partner should allow a peaceful dissolution of the marriage.

"Separates"

This word means "to separate oneself, to divorce." In the writings of the papyri, this word was used as a technical expression for divorce. If the unbeliever takes this initiative, then the believer is not bound. "Willful desertion of the unbeliever sets the other free, a case not contemplated in Christ's words in Matt. 5:32; 19:9. Luther argued that the Christian partner, thus released, may marry again. But that is by no means clear, unless the unbeliever marries first" (A. T. Robertson, *Word Pictures in the New Testament*, "Epistles of Paul," vol. 4, 128).

The meaning of verse 14 is not entirely clear. J. W. MacGorman comments, "Certainly Paul was not teaching the salvation of a pagan by marriage to a Christian as an alternative to faith in Christ. Nevertheless the marriage of a Christian and a pagan had a quality not to be found in the marriage of two pagans. Somehow and in some sense, through the intimate association of marriage to a believer, the unbeliever was consecrated. And thus their children were holy. A benefit is described, though its precise nature and extent are not defined" (*Romans, 1 Corinthians*, Layman's Bible Book Commentary [Nashville: Broadman & Holman Publishers, 1980], 121). *The New English Bible* uniquely renders this passage, "Think of it: as a wife you may be your husband's salvation; as a husband you may be your wife's salvation."

■ *Where only one spouse is a believer, a ques-*
■ *tion arises whether the two should continue*
■ *in the marriage relationship. Paul's first*
■ *principle is that the initiative belongs to the*
■ *unbeliever. If it is the desire of the unbeliev-*
■ *ing spouse to continue in the marriage, then*
■ *the Christian partner is to comply (vv. 12,*
■ *13). If the unbelieving spouse desires to sep-*
■ *arate, the Christian partner should allow a*
■ *peaceful dissolution of the marriage*

God Calls Us to Live in Peace (vv. 17–24)

Paul's second principle for dealing with a marriage where only one spouse is a believer is that "God has called us to live in peace" (v. 15). Paul's statement in verse 15 supports his instruction for Christians not to oppose an unbelieving spouse's determination to end the marriage. Verses 17–24 are an elaboration of his emphasis of verse 15. Paul then applied this principle to circumcision and slavery.

A religious application: circumcision (vv. 17–19). Whether circumcised or uncircumcised, a person should not seek to change his or her state.

A social application: slavery (vv. 20–24). Many slaves responded to the gospel and became believers. Whether a slave or a free person, one's status is not what matters. It is one's relationship to God that matters most.

■ *Paul exhorted the Corinthians to continue in*
■ *the state they were in when they were called*
■ *to Christ. Conditions of life are secondary.*
■ *Obedience to God is of primary importance.*

COUNSEL FOR THE UNMARRIED AND WIDOWS (7:8, 9, 25–40)

In verse 8, Paul repeated his statement that singleness is preferable to marriage. In this passage, Paul identified several tensions associated with this issue.

The Moral Tension (vv. 8, 9)

Paul began by advising unmarried and widows to remain single. He stated, however, that "it is better to marry than to burn with passion." Being married does not eliminate one's struggle with sexual temptation, but a good marriage is a strong defense against sexual immorality.

The "End Times" Tension (vv. 25–31)

It is clear from his writings that Paul believed that he was living in the time that would precede the end of the world. In this passage alone he made three allusions (vv. 26, 29, 31). In view of the "present crisis," Paul advised single believers not to seek a mate, but to remain as he or she was.

The Domestic Tension (vv. 32–35)

In verses 32 and 34, Paul presented a rather idealistic view of an unmarried man and woman. Both are devoting their full energies to the Lord's work. On the other hand, he portrayed the married as having divided interests. Paul sees a married woman as "concerned about the affairs of this world and how to please her husband" (v. 34).

Obviously, Paul's point is relative. The Christian man or woman who has no family responsibilities is free to devote more time and energy to ministry. But certainly not all Christian couples fit the pattern of distraction Paul describes here (see Priscilla and Aquila, Rom. 16:3–5).

"Virgin"

This word refers to either a father and his daughter or to a man and woman who have entered upon a spiritual marriage and now live together without physical relations, or a case of levirate marriage and the word means "young widow," or it refers to a man and woman who are an engaged couple. (Taken from Fritz Rienecker, *Linguistic Key to the Greek New Testament* [Grand Rapids: Zondervan, 1980], 410).

Individual Cases (vv. 36–38)

Paul now addressed individual cases involving virgins. There is some debate over the proper translation and interpretation of these verses, which makes this a difficult passage in some respects.

Remarriage for Widows (vv. 39, 40)

According to Paul, a wife is bound to her husband for as long as he lives. However, if he dies, she is free to remarry another man, "but he must belong to the Lord" (v. 39). Paul, however, believed that she is happier if she remains a widow.

■ *After repeating his statement that singleness is*
■ *preferable to marriage, Paul identified several*
■ *tensions associated with the issue of marrying*
■ *or remarrying. His conclusion was that "keep-*
■ *ing God's commands is what counts. Each one*
■ *should remain in the situation which he was in*
■ *when God called him." Paul also provided*
■ *instruction for virgins and widows.*

QUESTIONS TO GUIDE YOUR STUDY

1. What was Paul's concept of Christian marriage?
2. How should a believer handle a marriage where his or her spouse is not a believer?
3. What two principles govern the believer's decisions and actions?
4. What was Paul's counsel for unmarried Christians? For widows who are believers?

First Corinthians 8:1–11:1 is the unit of Paul's letter that deals with the issue of food sacrificed to idols. Chapter 8 reveals how Paul dealt with this problem in the church at Corinth in relation to varying levels of maturity among believers in the congregation.

THE ISSUE OF EATING FOOD OFFERED TO IDOLS (8:1–3)

In the pagan temples at Corinth, animal sacrifices were offered to gods. Only certain portions of the animal were used for this purpose, leaving the greater portion of the animal to be consumed by the priests and worshipers in a cultic meal. Following the sacrifices, the magistrates sold whatever remained to the local butcher shops. Because this was often the best meat available, those having dinner parties would be sure to purchase this meat and serve it to guests.

Paul addressed several questions here: What is the Christian's responsibility in such a setting? If invited to participate in a cultic meal at a pagan temple, should a believer attend? Was a believer permitted to buy meat that had been consecrated in pagan worship? If invited to the home of a pagan friend, was the believer free to accept the invitation? To refuse to attend such gatherings was to cut oneself off from social activity with friends. Differences of opinion among the Corinthian believers caused division within the church.

In verse 3 Paul explained that *love*, not *knowledge*, is the basis for Christian conduct. He then contrasted the two: "Knowledge puffs up, but love builds up." Knowledge, untempered by other qualities, fosters pride and arrogance. It can never

"Knowledge puffs up . . . love builds up"

"Knowledge puffs up." Paul's use of knowledge is not something purely intellectual. It is the knowledge that has results and leads to action, especially religious action. "Puff up" means "to blow up like a billows." Applied to an individual, this word means "to be inflated with self-complacency," "to make conceited." Because it is in the present tense, this verb emphasizes that what Paul said here is a general truth.

"Love builds up." The Greek word used here is a compound made up of the noun "house" and the verb "to build." Its basic meaning is applied to the building of something. It is the word used for describing the erection of buildings. Paul used it here as a metaphor for the development of Christian character.

be the only criterion as the guide to right conduct. But love never fosters pride and arrogance. Instead, it edifies or builds up the church.

Love, Not Knowledge, Is the Guide

	KNOWLEDGE	LOVE
What it does	"Puffs up"	"Builds up"
What it causes	Pride and arrogance	Character development
Its effects	Temporary	Permanent

■ *Paul dealt with the issue of eating food*
■ *offered to pagan idols. This issue raised sev-*
■ *eral questions, including: Was a believer per-*
■ *mitted to buy meat that had been consecrated*
■ *in pagan worship? In such complex issues,*
■ *Paul taught that love, not knowledge, is the*
■ *basis for Christian conduct.*

THE KNOWLEDGE OF THE MATURE BELIEVERS (8:4–6)

Paul addressed the mature members of the Corinthian congregation. In verse 4 he acknowledged their understanding about idols:

1. *"We know that an idol is nothing at all in the world."* There was no shortage of pagan gods in the ancient world. Their images and shrines were abundant. However, some Corinthian believers felt more mature because they knew that these idols didn't exist.

2. *"There is no God but one."* This statement reinforces a fundamental teaching of the Jewish

religion. In the *Shema*, the Jewish confession of faith, Deuteronomy 6:4 teaches that "the LORD our God, the LORD is one." This expression of faith may have been an early Christian confession. (Later worship practice combined Deut. 6:4–9; 11:13–21; Num. 15:37–41 into the larger Shema as the summary of Jewish confession.)

Because an idol represents something that does not exist, meat consecrated to it could not profane anyone. It remained simply meat, neither more nor less. This meant that the mature Christian could buy it and eat it with no defilement whatever. Christian liberty renders meaningless all such superstitions.

■ *Paul addressed the mature members of the*
■ *Corinthian congregation and acknowledged*
■ *their understanding about idols. Because an*
■ *idol represents something that did not exist,*
■ *the consecrated meat could not profane any-*
■ *one. Therefore, the mature Christian could*
■ *buy it and eat it with no defilement whatever.*

THE LIMITATIONS OF THE IMMATURE BELIEVERS (8:7–12)

Paul reminded his readers that not all members of the congregation were at the same level of understanding. As is often said today, "perception is reality." There were Christians who came out of a pagan background. Their consciences were weak. They had believed in pagan gods. When they turned to the living God, they turned away from the gods they had worshiped, but they could not yet think of them as not existing. So, when they thought of eating meat offered to these idols, they felt guilty. When they saw other Christians eating this meat, they were offended.

In verse 8 there is a hint that some of the mature believers may have been flaunting their freedom to eat such food, supposing that God esteemed them more highly for doing so. Paul refuted such thinking—"Food does not bring us near to God."

In 1 Corinthians, Paul addressed the issue of personal freedom concerning the eating of meat sacrificed to pagan idols. In chapter 8, he addressed the first limitation.

Paul's Three Limitations to Personal Freedom in 1 Corinthians

LIMITATION	FOCUS	PASSAGE
1. Paul indicated that one Christian should never eat meat if the eating offends a weaker Christian.	A weaker Christian	8:13
2. Paul suggested that a believer should limit the right to eat meat if that freedom hindered the spread of the gospel.	The spread of the gospel	9:19–23
3. Paul warned that a Christian should never indulge the freedom to eat meat if that action threatens the personal spiritual life of the individual.	One's own spiritual life	9:24–27

■ *Paul reminded his readers that not all mem-*
■ *bers of the congregation are at the same level*
■ *of understanding. And, some of the mature*
■ *believers may have been flaunting their free-*
■ *dom to eat such food, supposing that God*
■ *esteemed them more highly for doing so. Paul*
■ *taught that one Christian should never eat*
■ *meat if the eating offends a weaker Christian.*

LOVE'S REQUIREMENT (8:13)

Paul summed up his principle of self-limitation for the sake of others with the statement, "Therefore, if what I eat causes my brother to fall into sin, I will never eat meat again, so that I will not cause him to fall." The strong believer must adapt to the conscience of the weaker believer.

QUESTIONS TO GUIDE YOUR STUDY

1. The issue of eating food offered to pagan idols raised several questions for the Corinthians. What were some of those?

2. What did the mature believers at Corinth understand about idols that Paul agreed with? How had some of them crossed the line and erred with newer believers?

3. According to Paul, what is the basis for Christian conduct? Contrast love and knowledge.

4. What is love's requirement? Can you think of ways mature believers today might apply this principle in your church?

The Greek word translated *rights* can also be translated *freedom*.

In the preceding chapter Paul urged his mature readers to exercise their Christian freedom in a responsible way. In life, Paul practiced the principles he described.

He next devoted an entire chapter to a personal account of his own efforts to live on the level he recommended to his readers. Paul emphasized that one should subordinate one's own interests to those of others, especially those of Christ and His gospel. He identified four areas in which concerns for others led him to renounce or limit his rights:

- marriage (v. 5),
- financial support (vv. 4, 6–18),
- cultural bias (vv. 19–23), and
- self-discipline (vv. 24–27).

PAUL'S RIGHTS (9:1–3)
Paul began this chapter by defending his apostleship. Apparently, some Corinthian believers were criticizing Paul. Although he could have claimed privileges such as financial support from the church for his work and ministry, he did not. Rather, he was a tentmaker and worked to provide his own support.

MARRIAGE (9:5)
Paul presented a rhetorical question: "Don't we have a right to take a believing wife along with us, as do the other apostles and the Lord's brothers and Cephas?" Paul was not expecting an answer or special information. It was his way of emphatically claiming that he did have a right to marry a Christian woman, but that he yielded that right out of consideration for his ministry to others.

FINANCIAL SUPPORT (9:4, 6–18)

Paul was sensitive about the issue of financial support in his relations with the Corinthians. Apparently, some in the congregation were ready to question his motives if he should accept financial support as a minister of the gospel. Paul gave his readers several evidences that established his right to receive such support:

1. *He gave examples from everyday life (v. 7).* The soldier does not serve at his own expense. A person who plants a vineyard eats some of the fruit himself, and one who tends a flock is entitled to some of the milk.

2. *He appealed to Scripture (vv. 8–12).* Paul cited Deut. 25:4 as an illustration of the principle that the person doing the work requires material support.

"Do not muzzle an ox while it is treading out the grain" (Deut. 25:4).

3. *He pointed to the prevailing custom in the temple service (v. 13).* Those who served at the altar shared in the sacrificial offerings (Num. 18:8–32; Deut. 18:1–8).

4. *He appealed to the teachings of Jesus (v. 14).* "In the same way, the Lord has commanded that those who preach the gospel should receive their living from the gospel." But Paul did not ask for a contribution from the Corinthians.

■ *Paul defended his rights to marriage and*
■ *financial support. Although he could have*
■ *claimed the privilege of financial support*
■ *from the church for his work and ministry,*
■ *he did not. He cited several evidences to*
■ *prove his right. Rather than take compensa-*
■ *tion from the Corinthians, he worked as a*
■ *tentmaker to raise his own support.*

"I have become all things"

Paul used an interesting play on words in verse 22: "I have become *all* things to *all* men so that by *all* possible means I might save *some*." (Italics added.) There is a pointed play on the word *all*, that I might save some. This was his goal and worth all the cost of adaptation" (A. T. Robertson, *Word Pictures in the New Testament*, "Epistles of Paul," vol. 4, 148).

CULTURAL BIAS (9:19–23)

Paul had a remarkable history of spreading the gospel throughout many lands and in the midst of various cultures. His success was due partly to his flexibility and his willingness to take risks in moving beyond his own culture. For example, Paul wrote, "To the Jews I became like a Jew, to win the Jews" (v. 20).

He had unusual skills in distinguishing between the nonessential and the essential as he proclaimed the gospel. He willingly adapted to the cultural bias of his listeners, and he did so without compromising the gospel. Indeed, Paul declared in verse 22, "I have become all things to all men so that by all possible means I might save some."

■ *Paul effectively spread the gospel in the*
■ *midst of various cultures. His success was*
■ *due partly to his flexibility and his willing-*
■ *ness to take risks in moving beyond his own*
■ *culture. Paul summed up his goal in this*
■ *statement: "I have become all things to all*
■ *men so that by all possible means I might*
■ *save some."*

"Competes"

This is the Greek verb *agonizomai*, from which we get our English words *agony* and *agonize*. It means "to engage in an athletic contest, to strive, to contend." Paul was talking about an all-out effort, not a halfhearted attempt. The Christian is always to give his or her best.

SELF-DISCIPLINE (9:24–27)

Paul turned his attention to one's struggle with bodily appetites. To illustrate the Christian's need for self-discipline, he drew upon the athletic arena. Because the Isthmian games were held in Corinth every two years, these kinds of illustrations were likely popular and communicated well to his readers.

The Runner (vv. 24, 25)

A runner subjected himself to strict and rigid training to prepare for the games. To the runner who wanted the victor's wreath, no amount of self-control for peak performance was too great a price a pay. Paul's argument was that the Christian should train even harder for a "crown that will last forever."

The Boxer (vv. 26, 27)

Here Paul pictured the Greek boxer. The trained boxer does not win by "beating the air." Paul insisted that he deals decisive blows to his body to bring it under control. The boxer keeps his appetites under submission lest he disqualify himself.

■ *Paul addressed a person's struggle with*
■ *bodily appetites. The believer needs to bring*
■ *his or her appetites under control. Paul used*
■ *the illustrations of the runner and boxer to*
■ *make his point.*

QUESTIONS TO GUIDE YOUR STUDY

1. Why did Paul "waive his rights" in the areas of marriage and financial support?
2. Paul gave his readers several evidences that established his right to receive such support. What were they?
3. Why was Paul so successful in spreading the gospel into so many different cultures?
4. What was the point of Paul's two illustration from the athletic games?

Typology in the Bible

Typology is the method of interpreting some parts of Scripture by seeing a pattern that an earlier statement sets up and by which a later is explained. Typology involves a correspondence, usually in one particular matter, between a person, event, or thing in the Old Testament with a person, event, or thing in the New Testament.

1. *Old Testament warnings.* Paul rehearsed the experiences of the people of Israel in the Exodus in their forty years in the desert. All the people participated in these experiences, but God was not pleased with most of them who died in the desert (1 Cor. 10). The majority were types or warning patterns (examples) for Christians (v. 6).

2. *Adam as a type of Christ.* Paul compared Adam and Christ (Rom. 5:12–21). He argued that Christ's deed was much more powerful than Adam's transgression. The one point of correspondence in the passage is the effect of the influence upon humankind.

Paul showed how the Israelites, despite their rights and privileges, suffered in the wilderness. Through the use of typological interpretation of Old Testament events, Paul warned the Corinthians not to grumble or dabble with idolatry. Thus, Paul pointed to the disastrous experiences of Israel following the Exodus from Egypt to jolt them out of their complacency and arrogance (vv. 1–13).

Spiritual fellowship at the Lord's Supper served as a stern reminder that the Corinthians should have nothing to do with idols. One cannot share simultaneously in the Lord's table and in the table of demons (vv. 14–22).

ISRAEL'S FOLLY (10:1–5)

Having experienced baptism and the Lord's Supper, the Corinthians felt that their standing with God was secure. They believed they could also harmlessly choose to participate in cultic meals in pagan temples. They were enjoying a false security, and Paul refuted them by recalling the experiences in the life of ancient Israel: (1) the Israelites "were baptized into Moses" (v. 2) and (2) they participated in their equivalent of the Lord's Supper (vv. 3, 4). In spite of these "assurances," God was not pleased "with most of them" and "their bodies were scattered over the desert" (v. 5).

■ *Having experienced baptism and the Lord's*
■ *Supper, the Corinthians felt that their stand-*
■ *ing with God was secure. But the security*
■ *they felt was false. Paul warned them by*
■ *recalling the experiences in the life of ancient*
■ *Israel, in which similar attitudes resulted in*
■ *God's displeasure.*

PAUL'S ADMONITION (10:6–13)

Paul pointed out that the Israelites' "assurances" did not guarantee them entrance into the Promised Land, and then he made the connection between the Israelites and the believers at Corinth: "Now these things occurred as examples to keep us from setting our hearts on evil things as they did" (v. 6). A. T. Robertson comments, "More exactly, an example for us" (A. T. Robertson, *Word Pictures in the New Testament*, "Epistles of Paul," vol. 4, 152).

The Sins of the Israelites and the Sins of the Corinthians

SIN	1 COR. 10	OLD TESTAMENT PASSAGE
Desiring evil	v. 6	Num. 11:4–34
Worshiping idols	v. 7	Exod. 32:1–6
Sexual immorality	v. 8	Num. 25:1–9
Putting the Lord to the test	v. 9	Num. 21:4–9
Grumbling	v. 10	Num. 16:1–50

If self-trust and self-will led to the results they did for the children of Israel, that should keep the Corinthians from setting their hearts on

"Grumble"

The meaning of the word *grumble* is "to murmur, grumble, say anything in a low tone." The word in Greek is spelled *gonguzo*, and is an onomatopoetic word, representing the significance by the sound of the word. We get our English word *gong* from this word. (Taken from *Vine's Complete Expository Dictionary of Old and New Testament Words* [Nashville: Thomas Nelson, 1996], 422).

"evil things as they did" (v. 6). The following verses show four examples of what caused Israel's demise in the desert. In presenting these examples, Paul provided several directives for the Corinthians.

"Do not be idolaters" (v. 7). The Corinthian believers were not to emulate the actions of the children of Israel in the desert. Idolatry among God's people exposes them to God's judgment.

"We should not commit sexual immorality" (v. 8). Paul instructed some of the members of the congregation to "cease practicing fornication as some were already doing (1 Cor. 6:11). The connection between idolatry and fornication was very close. . . . It was very true of Corinth where prostitution was part of the worship of Aphrodite" (A. T. Robertson, *Word Pictures in the New Testament*, "Epistles of Paul," vol. 4, 153).

"We should not test the Lord" (v. 9). The Corinthians were putting Christ to the test by eating at both the Lord's Supper and the table of demons.

"Do not grumble" (v. 10). In Num. 14 we find that each time the Israelites "grumbled," God sent a punishment. The point is that grumbling about God brings His judgment.

■ *Paul pointed out that the Israelites' "assur-*
■ *ances" did not guarantee them entrance into*
■ *the Promised Land, and then he made the con-*
■ *nection between the Israelites and the believ-*
■ *ers at Corinth: "These things occurred as*
■ *examples to keep us from setting our hearts on*
■ *evil things as they did." Paul instructed the*
■ *Corinthians to refrain from those sins that*
■ *brought judgment to the Israelites.*

WARNING TO FLEE IDOLATRY (10:14–22)

The word *therefore* is an important word, as it signals that Paul was bringing his preceding argument to a logical conclusion. Paul had urgent counsel regarding sins of immorality and idolatry. His warning was abrupt but absolute. Christians are to "flee from idolatry" (v. 14). He supported his command by describing the believer's experience in the observance of the Lord's Supper.

By partaking of the elements of the Lord's Supper, the bread and the cup, believers participate in the blood and body of Christ. Paul appealed to the meaning of Jewish sacrifices—"consider the people of Israel" (v. 18). Those who ate sacrifices were partners in the altar.

What pagans sacrifice, they offer to demons—not to God. Although pagan idols represent gods that do not exist, the worship of those gods involves the worship of demons. Paul's question was, How can a believer participate with Christ in the Lord's Supper and also commune with demons in a pagan cultic meal? (v. 21). Attempting such a thing is to "arouse

Paul then summed up the examples of the Israelites as warnings for Christians. The Corinthians were to take care not to be self-confident: "So, if you think you are standing firm, be careful that you don't fall!" (v. 12). The Corinthians were experiencing what is "common to man" (v. 13). Whatever temptation they might face, they need not fall, but could count on God's help. He is faithful and will provide them a way out so they can stand up under the temptation. "The 'way out' is always right there along with the temptation" (A. T. Robertson, *Word Pictures in the New Testament*, "Epistles of Paul," vol. 4, 154). These truths are a comfort and source of strength to all Christians in all ages.

the Lord's jealousy" (v. 22) and invite the kind of judgment that fell on idolatrous Israel in the wilderness.

■ *Paul issued a direct and abrupt warning to*
■ *the Corinthians. They were to "flee from idol-*
■ *atry" (v. 14) and seek safety in flight. He sup-*
■ *ported his command by describing the*
■ *believer's experience in the observance of the*
■ *Lord's Supper. A believer cannot participate*
■ *with Christ in the Lord's Supper and also*
■ *commune with demons in a pagan cultic meal.*

SPECIFIC INSTRUCTIONS (10:23–11:1)

Note: Because it is obviously part of Paul's discussion in chapter 10, 1 Corinthians 11:1 is included here.

Paul began this section by repeating a catch-phrase he used in 6:12: "Everything is permissible." And, as in chapter 6, he added a qualifier, "But not everything is constructive." Christian liberty is important, but actions that do not build up or help others should be avoided.

Paul closed his discussion with specific instructions about Christian liberty and the eating of meat offered to pagan idols.

At the Meat Market (vv. 25, 26)

Believers were to go ahead and buy any meat sold in the meat market. It was impossible to know for certain whether any piece of meat had been offered to idols. Ultimately, it does not matter, for idols represent gods that do not exist. Paul's reasoning was that "the earth is the Lord's and everything in it" (v. 26). All meat is a provision from God, and because of its origin,

Christians may eat whatever meat they purchase at the meat market.

At an Unbeliever's Home (vv. 27, 28)

Christians were often dinner guests in the homes of unbelievers. Paul's instruction for this contingency was to eat what was served, "without raising questions of conscience" (v. 25). If, however, a fellow believer present took offense at eating meat that had been offered in sacrifice to idols, the other believer was not to eat the meat, in deference to the fellow believer's conscience.

GOD'S GLORY, THE PRIORITY (10:31–11:1)

Paul left this issue by providing the following instructions to his readers.

Whatever you do, do it for the glory of God (v. 31). Paul delivered this all-encompassing principle to his readers: "So whether you eat or drink or whatever you do, do it all for the glory of God" (v. 31).

Don't be a stumbling block to others (v. 32). Paul specifically mentions Jews, Greeks, and those who are part of the church.

"Follow my example" (11:1). As he often did, Paul appealed to himself as his readers' example. Because his example imitated Christ, they were to imitate Paul.

"This is the ruling motive in the Christian's life, not just having his own way about whims and preferences" (A. T. Robertson, *Word Pictures in the New Testament*, "Epistles of Paul," vol. 4, 158).

■ *Paul closed his discussion with specific*
■ *instructions about Christian liberty and the*
■ *eating of meat offered to pagan idols. Believ-*
■ *ers should go ahead and buy any meat sold in*
■ *the meat market. But in the event that a fellow*
■ *believer present took offense at eating meat*
■ *that had been offered in sacrifice to idols, the*
■ *other believer was not to eat the meat, in*
■ *deference to the fellow believer's conscience.*
■ *In all matters, the all-encompassing principle*
■ *is to do everything for the glory of God.*

QUESTIONS TO GUIDE YOUR STUDY

1. What was Israel's folly? Why did Paul remind the Corinthians of it?

2. What is a Bible type? What is its purpose? What did Paul intend to teach by using typology?

3. What does it mean to "grumble"? Why does this behavior bring God's judgment?

4. Some of the Corinthians struggled with idolatry. What was Paul's instruction to them? What modern-day applications might we find for his instruction?

5. Regarding the eating of meat offered to pagan idols, what principle did Paul give the Corinthians? Can you think of ways this principle is to be applied in today's church?

Paul turned his attention to matters of public worship. Every church bears witness to its faith through public services of worship. For this reason, Christian congregations need to be sensitive to the impressions they make upon the communities in which they serve.

In this chapter, Paul brought to the attention of the Corinthians an area in which they needed his guidance. Some of the activities of the church were causing disturbances and discrediting the testimony of the church:

- Women were flouting prevailing customs by participating in public worship with uncovered heads (vv. 2–16).
- Some members were profaning the observance of the Lord's Supper by shameful conduct (vv. 17–34).
- Those who spoke in tongues were dividing the church by their exaggerated and erroneous claims regarding their gift (12:1–14:40).

Note: Because 11:1 is part of the discussion of chapter 10, we begin the discussion of chapter 11 with verse 2.

THE VEILING OF WOMEN (11:2–16)

Certain women in the church at Corinth were creating a disturbance by failing to wear veils. Some of the Corinthian Christian women perhaps understood Paul's emphasis on Christian freedom to mean that they no longer had to observe any of the old Jewish customs—including wearing a veil. The effects of a such change had been disruptive to the worship services and the church's Christian witness in Corinth. This led Paul to state that a woman should cover her

Covering the Head

The Jewish custom for all women was to show modesty and virtue by covering their heads with a veil when they went outside their homes. The veiling of a woman's head was not a new concept for the Corinthians. In Jewish synagogues it was required, and in Greek sanctuaries women were also to be veiled. It is likely that the women in the Corinthian congregation were simply reflecting the more daring styles of the day.

The principle here is that Christians must be sensitive to the cultures in which they live and not needlessly flout local customs unless there is some moral reason to do so.

head during the worship service. At the same time, he encouraged the men to follow the Jewish custom of worshiping with uncovered heads. Paul cited several reasons for this teaching:

1. *The order of creation (v. 3)*. Woman comes below man in the divine order and should wear the head covering as a sign of subjection.
2. *The social customs of the time (vv. 4–6)*. An unveiled woman, like a woman with a shaved head, was looked down upon in disgrace.
3. *The presence of angels (v. 10)*. It is not certain what Paul meant here. Possibly he meant that if people are shocked by the presence of veiled women in services of worship, how much *more* the angels.
4. *Nature itself (vv. 13–15)*. Nature teaches that long hair is degrading to a man but commendable in a woman. That is, nature gives women longer hair than it does men. Paul did not specify precise length, as it was not important. He simply stated that it is longer and this is accepted as "her glory" (v. 15).
5. *The prevailing practice in churches (v. 16)*. Paul indicated that this practice was also observed elsewhere—"the churches of God."

■ *Some women in the church at Corinth were*
■ *creating a disturbance by failing to wear a*
■ *veil. Paul stated that a woman should cover*
■ *her head during the worship service. At the*
■ *same time, he encouraged the men to follow*
■ *the Jewish custom of worshiping with uncov-*
■ *ered heads.*

OBSERVANCE OF THE LORD'S SUPPER (11:17–34)

Some members were profaning the observance of the Lord's Supper by their shameful conduct. The following verses describe this problem.

Abuses Associated with Its Observance (vv. 17–22)

A fractured fellowship (vv. 18–20). Paul repeated a similar concern that he expressed in 1 Cor. 1:10–12. In that previous passage, divisions had arisen from conflicting loyalties to different leaders. Here the divisions were issuing from differences in economic and social status.

Disorder (v. 21). In addition to general disorder ("Each of you goes ahead without waiting for anybody else") Paul also cited instances of gluttony and drunkenness. Members were gorging themselves with food and getting drunk at the Lord's Supper.

Paul responded to these abuses with a series of rhetorical questions, which he used to hammer at the evils of their practice. Paul made it clear that he could not commend their actions: "What shall I say to you? Shall I praise you for this? Certainly not!"

Original Meaning of the Lord's Supper (vv. 23–26)

Because of the degree to which things had gotten out of hand at Corinth, Paul saw a need to remind his readers about the original meaning and purpose of the Lord's Supper. He began by describing the first Supper, as it had been reported by the earliest Christians.

"In remembrance of me" (vv. 23–25). Paul associated the Supper with the meal Jesus ate with His disciples "on the night he was betrayed" (v. 23).

The Lord's Supper

The Lord's Supper was a memorial celebrated by the early church to signify Jesus' sacrificial death for humankind's sin. The form of the observance was established by the Lord at the Last Supper—the Passover meal that Jesus shared with His disciples on the day before He was crucified. His actual death the following day fulfilled His words about His broken body and His shed blood. Only Paul uses the phrase "Lord's Supper" (1 Cor. 11:20), although this phrase is implied in Rev. 19:9 ("marriage supper of the Lamb"). Church fathers began to call the occasion the "Eucharist" (that is, "Thanksgiving") from the blessing pronounced over the bread and wine after about A.D. 100. Church groups celebrate the Lord's Supper regularly as a sign of the New Covenant sealed by Christ's death and Resurrection.

Written about A.D. 54 or 55, this letter brings us within three decades of the first Lord's Supper.

Participating in the Lord's Supper requires that we recall the extent to which Christ was willing to go to forgive us and make us what God intended from the beginning.

What would happen if every believer was acutely aware of God's love for him or her?

On this solemn occasion, Jesus gave thanks and then broke the bread, saying, "This is my body, which is for you; do this in remembrance of me" (v. 24).

Proclaiming "the Lord's death until he comes" (v. 26). When a congregation observes the Lord's Supper, it proclaims the gospel by its actions, and this proclamation of the Lord's death through the enactments of the Supper is to continue "until he comes." Even in the first century, the early Christians lived in the expectancy of the Lord's return. The observance of the Lord's Supper: (1) calls Christians to remember and proclaim Christ's sacrificial death on their behalf; (2) invites believers to celebrate His living presence; and (3) fixes the believers' hope upon the victory that His coming will bring.

The Need for Self-Examination (vv. 27–34)

Having provided background about the original meaning and purpose of the Lord's Supper, Paul returned to the situation that existed in the Corinthian church and their observance of this ordinance.

The word *therefore* (v. 27) is one Paul used to draw a conclusion. In this case, it introduced the consequence for the inappropriate behavior of the Corinthians. Whoever observes the Lord's Supper "in an unworthy manner will be guilty of sinning against the body and blood of the Lord."

Paul instructed the Corinthians to "examine" themselves before eating the bread and drinking the cup for the purpose of avoiding communicating unworthily (v. 27). Anyone who is unworthy while partaking of the Lord's Supper brings judgment. Paul stated that for this reason "many among you are weak and sick, and a number of you have fallen asleep" (v. 30). Here Paul noted that the ill health and even deaths of some of the Corinthians had spiritual causes.

Paul closed this part of his instruction by telling the Corinthians to wait for one another in the common meal and to satisfy their hunger at home.

- *The Lord's Supper should be a celebration of*
- *unity; instead, divisions among the church*
- *members were magnified. Because they were*
- *participating in Christ's body and blood, to*
- *participate in an unworthy manner profaned*
- *the Supper and invited judgment. Paul*
- *exhorted the Corinthians to examine their*
- *motives, methods, and manners when they*
- *gathered to worship the Lord at His supper.*

QUESTIONS TO GUIDE YOUR STUDY

1. Why did women veil their heads? Why was the veiling of a woman's head such an issue? How does Paul's teaching on this issue impact today's church?

2. What is the Lord's Supper? What is meant by the "bread" and the "cup"? What is the significance of this ordinance for the believer?

3. Why did Paul take issue with the Corinthians over their observance of the Lord's Supper?

4. How does one partake of the Lord's Supper worthily? What is the consequence for observing the Supper unworthily?

The exercise of spiritual (or charismatic) gifts in the church was a subject about which the Corinthians had asked for advice. Many of them were attracted by the more spectacular gifts. Chapters 12–14 provide the most extensive passage in the New Testament on charismatic gifts. These gifts had become a divisive issue in the church at Corinth. Some members regarded their own spiritual gifts with pride and exclusiveness.

"Speaking in Tongues"

The Greek word *glossolalia* refers to the gift of speaking in tongues. It involved the ability to speak in a foreign language (or languages) not previously studied or to respond to and experience of the Holy Spirit by uttering sounds that believers without the gift of interpreting tongues could not understand. At Corinth, some members of the church uttered sounds which the rest of the congregation did not understand (1 Cor. 12–14). This led to controversy and division. Paul tried to reunite the church, assuring the church that there are different gifts but only one Spirit (1 Cor. 12:4–11).

The Corinthians tended to place an extreme value on one the most dramatic of these gifts—speaking in tongues or *glossolalia*. The overemphasis of those who used this gift prompted the overreaction of those who did not speak in tongues. The result of the confusion over these gifts was further division.

Paul countered this crisis by raising questions about the problem of *glossolalia* with the following response pattern:

- He *taught* about the nature of the church as the body of Christ.
- He *appealed* to love as the more excellent way.
- He *confronted* those who spoke in tongues, who wrongly valued ecstatic utterance above prophetic utterance.

THE NATURE AND FUNCTION OF CHARISMATIC GIFTS (12:1–11)

"Jesus Is Lord" (vv. 1–3)

Paul established the ultimate test of the presence and power of the Spirit in the believer's life; it is the confession that "Jesus is Lord" (v. 3). The

Holy Spirit alone can plant this confession in a person's heart. Therefore, a church is the body of Christ, consisting of members who experience Him as Lord.

Enabling Graces (vv. 4–7)

As believers are saved by grace, so also are they equipped by grace to serve. Spiritual gifts are bestowed by the Holy Spirit upon every believer. In these verses Paul mentioned the varieties of spiritual gifts, emphasizing that each has the same divine source and operation. His statement in verse 7, "To each one the manifestation of the Spirit is given for the common good," provides two key points for the reader:

1. This means that every Christian receives some gift or enabling grace. No believer is overlooked when it comes to receiving a spiritual gift.
2. Gifts are given by the Holy Spirit to individual members for the good of the entire congregation. They equip members of the church to function as the body of Christ in a community.

Paul is clear that to regard a spiritual gift as a merit badge to designate God's elite or as evidence of total commitment is to misunderstand the purpose of the giving of these enabling gifts.

■ *As believers are saved by grace, so also are*
■ *they equipped by grace to serve. The*
■ *enabling grace, or spiritual gifts, is bestowed*
■ *by the Holy Spirit upon every believer. Paul*
■ *emphasizes that each gift has the same divine*
■ *source and operation.*

The Charismatic Gifts (vv. 8–11)

The gifts listed (vv. 8–10). Paul named a representative list of nine charismatic gifts:

LISTING OF GIFTS IN 1 CORINTHIANS 12:8–11

1. wisdom	6. prophecy
2. knowledge	7. the ability to distinguish between spirits
3. faith	8. tongues
4. gifts of healing	9. interpretation of tongues
5. working of miracles	

Other New Testament passages that include some spiritual gifts or offices not mentioned here are 1 Corinthians 7:7; 12:28; Romans 12:6–8; Ephesians 4:11. (For an exhaustive list of gifts, see the chart, "Paul's Lists of Spiritual Gifts," in the introduction.)

The sovereignty of the Spirit (v. 11). The giving of spiritual gifts is not a "do-it-yourself" operation. Only the Holy Spirit can give these gifts. "All these are the work of one and the same Spirit, and he gives them to each one, just as he determines." As a result, no Christian can boast that he or she has accomplished or attained his or her gift.

■ *In this passage, Paul listed some of the char-*
■ *ismatic gifts. He emphasized that the source*
■ *of each gift is the Holy Spirit: "All of these*
■ *are the work of one and the same Spirit."*

THE INTERDEPENDENCE OF CHARISMATIC GIFTS (12:12–31)

Baptism in the Spirit

Baptized into One Body (vv. 12, 13)

Paul used the analogy of the body to describe the church. The body has many different members and organs, yet these unique parts all work together to form the body. Paul applied this analogy to the body of believers: "So it is with Christ. For we were all baptized by one Spirit into one body—whether Jews or Greeks, slave or free—and we were all given the one Spirit to drink."

With his phrase, "We were all baptized by one Spirit into one body," Paul did not use this word to refer to water baptism, but rather spiritual transformation that puts the believer "in Christ." It is the effect of receiving the gift of the Spirit that takes place at the time of the believer's conversion.

As the body of Christ, the church is a unit of solidarity that transcends all ethnic and social distinctions (Gal. 3:27, 28; Col. 3:11).

The Folly of Discord Within the Body (vv. 14–26)

Paul now turned to a method of argument that showed the Corinthians how ridiculous their discord was. He made two points.

1. *Paul imagined a dissatisfied foot and a proud ear (vv. 15–20).* The foot wants to be a hand, and the ear wants to be an eye. Because they are both unable to arrange such trades, they declare their intentions to secede from the body. Paul responded: "But in fact God has arranged the parts in the body, every one of them, just as he wanted them to be" (v. 18).

2. *Paul imagined a proud eye and a proud head (vv. 21–26).* The proud eye scorns the hand, and the head scorns the feet. Paul maintained that this is folly, as all parts of the body unite in a remarkable interdependence. Each part is unique and essential. Paul explained, "Those parts of the

body that seem to be weaker are indispensable" (v. 22).

In this passage, Paul taught these important truths about the body of Christ:

1. There should be no division within the body (v. 25).
2. If one part of the body suffers, the whole body suffers with it (v. 26).
3. If one part of the body is honored, the whole body rejoices with it (v. 26).

The God-Appointed Ministries of the Church (vv. 27–31)

Paul took his analogy of the body and applied it directly to the church at Corinth: "Now you are the body of Christ" (v. 27). Some of the members of the congregation were building a fellowship around the gift of tongues and, in doing so, they were denying the nature of the church as the body of Christ.

He then cited God's appointments in the church to various ministries:

MINISTRIES OF THE CHURCH	
1. apostles	5. healers
2. prophets	6. helpers
3. teachers	7. administrators
4. workers of miracles	8. speakers in tongues

Paul presented seven rhetorical questions to make a point that no Christian has all these charismatic gifts and that no one gift is bestowed upon all.

Verse 31, "But eagerly desire the greater gifts," serves as a transition that points to chapter 13.

■ *Paul took his analogy of the body and*
■ *applied it directly to the church at Corinth.*
■ *He cited God's appointments in the church to*
■ *various ministries, emphasizing that no*
■ *Christian has all these charismatic gifts and*
■ *that no one gift is bestowed upon all.*

QUESTIONS TO GUIDE YOUR STUDY

1. What is the gift of "speaking in tongues"?
2. Why did Paul take issue with some believers at Corinth who spoke in tongues?
3. From this portion of Paul's letter, what do we learn about the nature of spiritual gifts? About the proper exercise of these gifts?
4. In 12:12–21, what important truths does Paul teach about the body of Christ?

"If..."

In verses 1–3, the word *if* introduces what is known as a *condition*. Conditional constructions in the New Testament have four functions, one of which is to show the possibility of something occurring. That was Paul's intent here. Four times he used this grammatical construction to drive home the point that the proper use of the gifts of the Spirit is conditional. Indeed, it is possible for believers to use the gifts of the Spirit without bringing honor to God and building the church. Unless they are exercised as expressions of love, the gifts become meaningless and gain nothing.

Paul explained the proper way to exercise all spiritual gifts. He now showed the supreme fruit of the Spirit—a more excellent way.

LOVE: THE MORE EXCELLENT WAY (13:1–13)

The Necessity of Love (vv. 1–3)

How important is love? Christians may be talented, gifted, devoted, generous in their giving, or endowed with mountain-moving faith; but those are of no value if love is not present. Without love, none of the gifts can honor God and build up the church.

Paul presented four conditions that embrace very important concepts of Christianity to show the meaninglessness of using the gifts without love.

The gift of tongues (v. 1). No earthly or heavenly language compares with the exercise of love. The use of tongues without interpretation has no meaning. If it is exercised without love, it results in nothing more than noise—"a resounding gong" or "clanging cymbal."

The gift of prophecy (v. 2a). "All knowledge" means the sum of all wisdom, both human and divine. "Mysteries" have to do with those things we cannot know without revelation from God. Even if a person were able to fathom all this—without the expression of love—it would amount to nothing.

The gift of faith (v. 2b). If a person were to exercise the kind of faith that works miracles and use it to its fullest extent, but lacked love, the use of this gift would have no value.

The gift of giving (v. 3). Acts of giving and self-sacrifice, if not done in love, accomplish nothing. Even if one were to surrender one's "body to the flames," if it is not done within the context of love, it is worthless.

In this passage, Paul used the phrase "but have not love." He did not refer to a possession of love but to the idea of "acting lovingly."

Without Love...

"If..."	Apparent Worth	Result
If I speak in tongues	of men and angels	I am only a clanging cymbal
If I have the gift of prophecy	can fathom mysteries and all knowledge	I am nothing
If I have faith	that can move mountains	I am nothing
If I give all I possess to the poor	surrender my body to the flames	I gain nothing

■ *Paul discussed the necessity of love in the*
■ *exercise of the charismatic gifts. Christians*
■ *may be talented, gifted, devoted, generous in*
■ *their giving, or endowed with mountain-*
■ *moving faith; but those are of no value if love*
■ *is not present. Without love, none of the gifts*
■ *can honor God and build up the church.*

THE CHARACTERISTIC ACTIONS OF LOVE (VV. 4–7)

Paul made it clear that genuine love is active, not static. Love is something people *do*.

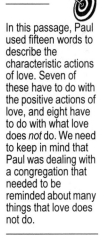

In this passage, Paul used fifteen words to describe the characteristic actions of love. Seven of these have to do with the positive actions of love, and eight have to do with what love does *not* do. We need to keep in mind that Paul was dealing with a congregation that needed to be reminded about many things that love does not do.

Patient

The church at Corinth had at least two kinds of people who had been wronged: those involved in lawsuits and the poor who were made to feel their poverty at church meals. Love, on their part, would show itself as patience—not retaliating when wronged.

Seven Positive Actions of Love

1. *It is patient (v. 4).* One who is patient waits a long time before giving room to action or passion. It is the opposite of one who is short-tempered.

2. *It is kind (v. 4).* Kindness is being gracious and useful to others.

3. *It rejoices with the truth (v. 6).* Love rejoices in the truth of God and the gospel. The loving person rejoices with that which reflects the gospel, such as the forgiveness of sins and acts of kindness toward others.

4. *It always protects (v. 7).* Love covers. It conceals what is unbecoming or displeasing in another rather than bringing that person's "dirty laundry" out into full view of others.

5. *It always trusts (v. 7).* Although love is not to be gullible or deceived by pretense, it does allow for circumstances and actions in others, and it tries to see the best in them.

6. *It always hopes (v. 7).* Love always has the forward look, no matter the circumstances. It never loses hope because it never ceases to have faith.

7. *It always perseveres (v. 7).* Love is not overwhelmed by circumstances, but it continues in spite of difficulty.

Eight Negative Actions of Love

1. *It does not envy (v. 4).* Love avoids acts of jealousy and envy toward others. It is not upset or displeased when others succeed.

2. *It does not boast (v. 4).* One who loves does not assert oneself. A loving person is not arrogant or boastful. The Greek word

Paul used here means to behave as a braggart or "wind-bag."

3. *It is not proud (v. 4).* Love does not cause one to be puffed up; it is not addicted to the sin of pride.

4. *It is not rude (v. 5).* A loving person is tactful and refrains from behaving indecently or in a shameful manner.

5. *It is not self-seeking (v. 5).* Love is not self-centered. It does not seek to have its own way.

6. *It is not easily angered (v. 5).* A loving person is not "touchy" or easily irritated. Such a person is not provoked to anger by others.

7. *It keeps no record of wrongs (v. 5).* A loving person does not keep accounts of wrongdoing. Neither does a loving person take notice of every evil thing another does and then hold it against that person.

8. *It does not delight in evil (v. 6).* Love does not take pleasure or satisfaction in evil of any kind.

■ *In this passage, Paul used fifteen words to*
■ *describe the characteristic actions of love.*
■ *Seven of these have to do with the positive*
■ *actions of love, and eight have to do with*
■ *what love does not do.*

THE SUPREMACY OF LOVE (13:8–13)

Love Never Fails (v. 8)

Paul makes a bold statement: "Love never fails" (v. 8). This means that love is never defeated. Nothing can cause it to collapse. He then contrasts love with the spiritual gifts. Love is greater than the gifts because it is *eternal* and the gifts are *temporal*.

Whereas love never ends, the temporal gifts will eventually disappear:

- prophecies will cease,
- tongues will be stilled, and
- knowledge will pass away.

The Complete vs. the Partial (vv. 9–12)

These verses explain what Paul had asserted in verse 8 and serve to illustrate the temporality of the gifts and the eternality of love.

Paul stated that when "perfection comes, the imperfect disappears" (v. 10). In verses 11, 12, Paul continued with two analogies that contrast the *partial* with the *complete*.

Mirrors

"A city like Corinth, famous for its bronze mirrors, would have particularly appreciated Paul's final illustration. The perfection and imperfection mentioned in verse 10 were deftly likened to the contrasting images obtained by the indirect reflection of one's face viewed in a bronze mirror and the same face when viewed directly." From *The Bible Knowledge Commentary, New Testament* (Zondervan), 536.

Human growth (v. 11). Paul likened the imperfection of this present age with the perfection of the future by his analogy of human growth. As children grow up, their actions, speech, and thoughts mature. They put "childish ways" behind them.

A mirror (v. 12). The Christian's knowledge of God at present may be compared to the imperfect reflection of an ancient metal mirror. However, in eternity the believer's knowledge of God will be "face to face." The believer's partial understanding will yield to a full understanding of God.

The Three Great Realities (v. 13)

Paul closed this chapter with a brief discussion of the three great realities that will endure forever. These enduring realities are faith, hope, and love. Of the three, Paul said, "the greatest of these is love."

The Three Great Realities

REALITY	WHY THEY ENDURE
Faith	Because the believer's relationship to God will always be one of trust and commitment
Hope	Because the believer will participate with God in an eternal order that is dynamic
Love	Because where God is, love is

- *Paul stated that "love never fails." As he con-*
- *trasted genuine love with spiritual gifts, he*
- *showed that love is greater that the gifts*
- *because it is eternal, whereas the gifts are*
- *temporal. Paul closed this chapter with a brief*
- *discussion of the three great realities that will*
- *endure forever: faith, hope, and love.*

QUESTIONS TO GUIDE YOUR STUDY

1. Why is love necessary in the exercise of spiritual gifts?
2. Paul mentioned seven positive characteristics of love. What are they, and what does each contribute to the building up of the body of Christ?
3. Paul mentioned eight negative characteristics of love. What are they, and what does each contribute to the building up of the body of Christ?
4. What are the three realities that endure forever?

Paul declared that one reason why the gift of prophecy is more important than speaking in tongues is that it edifies the entire congregation. He used three words to describe how prophecy ministers to believers in the church.

Strengthening. This word is a compound made up of the noun "a home" and the verb "to build," and denotes the act of building. Here it refers to the body of Christ and depicts the edification, the building up of others that is a result of the exercise of the gift of prophecy.

Encouragement. This is a compound made up of the words "by the side" and "to call," and means "a calling to one's aid." Here it refers to exhortation of one another in the body of Christ through the exercise of the gift of prophecy.

Comfort. This is yet another compound made up of the words *near* and *speech.* Literally, it means "a speaking closely to anyone." Here it refers to consolation and comfort that result from the exercise of the gift of prophecy within the body of Christ.

In this chapter Paul confronted the erroneous claims of those who spoke in tongues. He sought to point out their error by comparing the relative values of the two gifts: prophecy and speaking in tongues.

PROPHECY IS MORE IMPORTANT THAN TONGUES (14:1–25)

Definitions

The gift of prophecy. This gift has to do with Spirit-inspired utterance that is intelligible. It has a recognizable vocabulary through which God's message is communicated.

The gift of speaking in tongues. This gift is Spirit-inspired utterance that is *not* intelligible. It is a form of ecstatic utterance. It is *not* the ability to speak in foreign languages.

Paul informed the Corinthians that both the gifts of prophecy and speaking in tongues are valid spiritual gifts. However, they are not of equal importance in the ministries of the church. Whereas those speaking in tongues regarded their gift more highly than the other gifts, Paul taught that prophecy is more important. He gave the Corinthians three reasons:

1. Prophecy edifies the whole church.
2. Prophecy is understood by all.
3. Prophecy inspires conviction, confession, and worship.

Prophecy Edifies the Whole Church (vv. 1–12)

Speaking in tongues has a value, as does any gift bestowed by the Spirit. The Spirit alone determines the who, when, and where of all His gifts

(v. 4). However, in Corinth, and often since, *glossolalia* was magnified out of proportion to its value. Self-edification is its primary contribution. Unless accompanied by the gift of interpretation, it cannot build up the congregation (v. 5).

But prophecy is different. As speaking in tongues is ecstatic speech addressed to God by people, so prophecy is intelligible speech addressed by God through people to others. Paul claimed, "He who speak in tongues edifies himself, but he who prophesies edifies the church" (v. 4).

The Relative Value of Tongues and Prophecy

AREA OF CONTRAST	SPEAKING IN TONGUES	PROPHECY
Edification	Self-edifying	Edifies the entire congregation
Understanding	Needs to be interpreted to be understood	Understood by all who are listening
How message is communicated	From people to God	From God through people to others

- Although the gifts of prophecy and speaking
- in tongues were valid, they were not of equal
- importance in the ministries of the church.
- Whereas those speaking in tongues regarded
- their gift more highly than the other gifts,
- Paul taught that prophecy is more impor-
- tant. He provided three reasons to support
- his argument: (1) prophecy edifies the whole
- church; (2) prophecy is understood by all;
- and (3) prophecy inspires conviction, confes-
- sion, and worship.

Prophecy Is Understood by All (vv. 13–19)

"For this reason" refers to the goal of strengthening the church. Paul instructed the one who speaks in tongues to "pray that he may interpret what he says" (v. 13). The problem was that although a person who is praising God in tongues may be expressing genuine thanks, others may not know when to respond with an "Amen!" (v. 16).

Paul claimed that he spoke in tongues, but he placed greater value upon "five intelligible words to instruct others than ten thousand words in a tongue" (v. 18). This statement should be a reminder to believers not to exaggerate the value of the gift of speaking in tongues.

■ *Whereas speaking in tongues cannot be*
■ *understood by others, the gift of prophecy*
■ *can be understood by the entire congrega-*
■ *tion. This elevates the gift of prophecy to a*
■ *higher level of importance.*

Prophecy Inspires Conviction, Confession, and Worship (vv. 20–25)

Paul was concerned about the impact the exercise of these charismatic gifts had upon unbelievers. Here he contrasted the impressions prophecy and tongues had on those who were not Christians. He offered two kinds of responses from unbelievers:

1. Glossolalia *invites scorn (v. 23)*. Paul imagined a situation in which visitors are present at worship and everyone is speaking in tongues. What will they think? What value will they take away from this?

2. *Prophecy inspires worship (vv. 24, 25).* Clear communication, on the other hand, could bring conviction and could be used by the Spirit to bring the visitor to exclaim, "God is really among you!"

The point of Paul's contrast here was that the gift of prophecy that prompted them to worship God was superior to the gift of tongues that led unbelievers to respond with, "You are out of your mind."

- *Paul was concerned about the impact the exercise of these charismatic gifts had upon unbelievers. Here he contrasted the impressions prophecy and tongues have on those who are not Christians: speaking in tongues invites scorn, whereas prophecy inspires worship.*

PRACTICAL GUIDANCE IN WORSHIP (14:26–40)

Broad Principles (vv. 26, 33, 40)

Paul advocated orderly worship. Some of the Corinthians prized the more spectacular gifts, such as speaking in tongues, above all others. If the exercise of such gifts were not done in an orderly fashion, Christian worship and service could easily degenerate into an experience of frenzy and flamboyance with little moral substance. Paul's instructions in this section were designed to correct the abuses the Corinthians were allowing.

Specific Items (vv. 26, 27–32, 33–36)

The proper exercise of charismatic gifts (v. 26). Paul mentioned several activities of worship that take place when believers come together:

Paul equipped his readers with three basic principles that he applied to their worship and service:

1. "All of these must be done for the strengthening of the church" (v. 26).

2. "God is not a God of disorder, but of peace" (v. 33).

3. "Everything should be done in a fitting and orderly way" (v. 40).

- a hymn,
- a word of instruction,
- a revelation,
- a tongue, and
- an interpretation.

Controlling principle: All of these activities were to be exercised according to the principle in verse 26: "All of these must be done for the strengthening of the church."

The number of prophets or speakers in tongues who may take part in a service (vv. 27–32). At times, several members of the congregation at Corinth exercised the gift of tongues *simultaneously*, making for confusion. Paul taught that prophecy also needs to be regulated; that no more than "two or three prophets" should speak in a service. The purpose was that all might be instructed and encouraged.

Controlling principle: "God is not a God of disorder, but of peace" (v. 33).

Restrictions upon the participation of women (vv. 33–36). Paul instructed women to "remain silent in the churches" (v. 34). The context of this passage does not discuss whether women were qualified to minister, but rather was concerned with how they should learn (v. 35). Paul instructed his readers, "If they want to inquire about something, they should ask their own husbands at home" (v. 35).

It should be noted that Paul asked the Corinthians to conform to what was the accepted Christian practice of his day. In the eyes of most people, women assuming the role of instructor or teacher would have been a discredit to Christianity. Among the Greeks, for example, women were discouraged from saying anything in public. The Jews even regarded it a sin to teach a woman.

In verses 37–40, Paul closed this section by appealing to those who considered themselves prophets. All are to "be eager to prophesy" and "not forbid speaking in tongues" (v. 39).

Controlling principle: Whether the participation of women in the church or the exercise of spiritual gifts, Paul reminded his readers that "everything should be done in a fitting and orderly way" (v. 40).

■ *Paul advocated orderly worship, and his*
■ *instructions in this section were designed to*
■ *correct the abuses the Corinthians were*
■ *allowing. He centered his teaching on three*
■ *basic principles: (1) all must be done for the*
■ *purpose of strengthening of the church; (2)*
■ *the God they worship is not a God of disor-*
■ *der, but of peace; and (3) everything must be*
■ *done in an orderly way.*

QUESTIONS TO GUIDE YOUR STUDY

1. What are the gifts of *prophecy* and *speaking in tongues*?
2. Why is prophecy the more important of the two gifts?
3. Paul presented three controlling principles for worship and service. Describe them. How well are these applied in our churches today?
4. What were Paul's instructions regarding the role of women in the church? How are we to apply these to today's church?

In this chapter we have the earliest existing account of the Resurrection of Jesus Christ. Some believers in Corinth were saying that there was no resurrection of the dead. We do not know the details of this denial. Earlier in his letter, Paul rebuked the arrogant Corinthians for acting as though the consummation had already occurred and they were basking in its glories (4:8–13). Paul sought to refute the denial of the Resurrection by affirming the certainty of the Resurrection (vv. 1–34) and describing the nature of the resurrected body (vv. 35–38).

TESTIMONY OF THE EYEWITNESSES (15:1–11)

The gospel message that Paul understated has three vital emphases:

1. "Christ died for our sins according to the Scriptures" (v. 3).
2. "He was buried" (v. 4).
3. "He was raised on the third day according to the Scriptures (v. 4).

Following His Resurrection, Jesus appeared to several of His followers. Paul mentioned Jesus' post-resurrection appearances, capping his list with Paul's Damascus Road encounter.

- *Some believers in Corinth were saying that*
- *there was no resurrection of the dead. Paul*
- *refuted their denial of the Resurrection, cit-*
- *ing Jesus' post-resurrection appearances,*
- *capping his list with his own Damascus Road*
- *encounter with the resurrected Lord.*

Paul's Account of Jesus' Post-Resurrection Appearances

APPEARANCE	PASSAGE
1. Peter	Luke 24:34; Mark 16:7; John 21:1–14
2. The Twelve	Matt. 28:16–20; Luke 24:36–49; John 20:19–25
3. Five hundred believers	1 Cor. 15:6
4. James	1 Cor. 15:7
5. The apostles	1 Cor. 15:7
6. Paul	1 Cor. 15:8

DENIAL OF THE RESURRECTION (15:12–19)

Now Paul more directly challenged the denial of the Resurrection. Whether the Corinthians' denial of the resurrection included Jesus' Resurrection is not known. However, Paul's argument against the denial of resurrection constituted a denial of Jesus' Resurrection: "If there is no resurrection of the dead, then not even Christ has been raised" (v. 13).

Now for the sake of argument, Paul assumed that Jesus had not been raised from the dead, and proceeded to draw conclusions based upon this false premise:

1. *Preaching the truth, "our preaching is useless" (v. 14).* An unresurrected Christ would make Paul's preaching false witness.
2. *Faith without forgiveness, "your faith is futile; you are still in your sins" (v. 17).* If Jesus had remained a victim of sin and death following His Resurrection, He would have been unable to deliver us from the power of sin and death.
3. *Death without hope, "Then those also who have fallen asleep in Christ are lost" (v. 18).* The death of those who believed on

Christ's death, burial, and Resurrection served as the foundation of all Paul preached and wrote.

Christ have the same end as those who denied Him.

4. *Sacrifice without meaning, "If only for this life we have hope in Christ, we are to be pitied more than all men" (v. 19).* Christ's sacrifice was wasted on an illusion.

■ *Paul challenged the Corinthians' denial of*
■ *the Resurrection. For the sake of argument,*
■ *Paul assumed that Jesus has not been raised*
■ *from the dead, and drew four conclusions*
■ *based upon this false premise. Christ's death,*
■ *burial, and Resurrection were the foundation*
■ *of all Paul preached and wrote.*

CONSEQUENCES OF CHRIST'S RESURRECTION (15:20–28)

Paul now turned from drawing conclusions based upon the premise of an unresurrected Christ to an affirmation of faith. Christ indeed has been raised from the dead (v. 20), and is the "firstfruits of those who have fallen asleep."

Leviticus 23:4–11 is the background for the metaphor of the firstfruits. The waving of the sheaf of the firstfruits of the grain harvest before God consecrated the whole harvest to follow.

Drawing from that Old Testament concept, Paul taught that the Resurrection of Christ as the firstfruits of those who have died is the assurance that those who trust Christ shall have a resurrection like His.

In verses 23–26, Paul showed order in the Resurrection: Christ was the firstfruits; "then, when he comes, those who belong to him" (v. 23). The resurrection of believers is related to the second coming of Christ. "Then the end will

"Firstfruits"

This word means the first installment of the crop which foreshadows and pledges the ultimate offering of the whole. The word was used in various ways in the papyri: a birth certificate, a certificate of authorization, a yearly offering for a god, or an inheritance tax. (Taken from Fritz Rienecker, *Linguistic Key to the Greek New Testament* [Grand Rapids: Zondervan, 1980], 441).

come, when he hands over the kingdom to God the Father after he has destroyed all dominion, authority and power" (v. 24). And death, described as the last enemy, will be destroyed (v. 26).

■ *Paul now turned from drawing conclusions*
■ *based upon the premise of an unresurrected*
■ *Christ to an affirmation of faith. Christ*
■ *indeed has been raised from the dead (v. 20),*
■ *and is the "firstfruits of those who have fallen*
■ *asleep."*

OTHER ARGUMENTS FOR THE RESURRECTION (15:29–34)

For the sake of argument, Paul draws two more negative conclusions:

1. *Baptism on behalf of the dead is futile (v. 29).* "Now if there is no resurrection, what will those do who are baptized for the dead?" Although this is a puzzling verse, it probably refers to vicarious baptism, which is the baptizing of a person in place of another who died unbaptized.

2. *Risking one's life for the sake of the gospel is folly (v. 30).* "Why do we endanger ourselves every hour?" The apostles were in constant danger. Why should anyone endure the risks associated with Christianity if death is final?

THE NATURE OF THE RESURRECTED BODY (15:35–58)

The discussion of the nature of the resurrected body begins in verse 35 with two questions:

Biblical examples of the use of the word *firstfruits* include:

- Christ in His Resurrection is the "firstfruits" of those who sleep (1 Cor. 15:20, 23);
- the Holy Spirit is spoken of as "firstfruits" (Rom. 8:23);
- believers are also spoken of as "a kind of firstfruits" (Jas. 1:18);
- the saved remnant within Israel is described as "firstfruits" (Rom. 11:16);
- the 144,000 of the tribulation period are described as "firstfruits"(Rev. 14:4); and the converts of an area were designated "firstfruits" (Rom. 16:5; 1 Cor. 16:15).

"How are the dead raised?" and "With what kind of body will they come?"

Paul's response to those questions was, "How foolish! What you sow does not come to life unless it dies" (v. 36). He followed by presenting an analogy from nature and an appeal to Scripture.

Paul's Analogy from Nature (vv. 36–44)

Paul insisted that believers would experience resurrection with an imperishable body suited for life in the world beyond. His analogy from nature made the point that death is a transition to a higher life.

Grains and plants (vv. 36–38). Paul used the metaphor of a *seed*. A seed goes through stages:

- it is planted in the ground;
- it dies (germinates); and
- it yields a new body.

Men and animals (v. 39). Humans, animals, birds, and fish have different kinds of flesh. Through the idea that there are different kinds of flesh, Paul prepared the way in his readers' minds that there can indeed be a difference in the kind of body one has *before* the resurrection and the body one has *after* the resurrection.

The heavenly bodies (vv. 40, 41). In a smaller way, there is a difference between the heavenly bodies and earthly bodies. With the variety and adequacy with which God has clothed all kinds of celestial and terrestrial life, He should be able to provide suitable bodies for those who will share in the eternal order.

Application of the analogy (vv. 42–44). The phrase "so will it be" signaled to Paul's readers that Paul was now applying his analogy to the issue of the resurrection of the dead. "Paul now applies his illustrations to his argument to prove the kind of body we shall have after the resurrection. He does it by a series of marvelous contrasts that gather all his points. The earthly and the risen beings differ in duration, value, and power" (A. T. Robertson, *Word Pictures in the New Testament*, "Epistles of Paul," vol. 4, 196).

The Resurrection Body

	BEFORE—"SOWN"	AFTER—"RAISED"
Its duration	perishable	imperishable
Its value	dishonor	glory
Its power	weakness	power
Its nature	natural body	spiritual body

■ Paul discussed the nature of the resurrected
■ body by using an analogy from nature. His
■ observations of seeds, flesh, and the variety
■ and splendor of heavenly bodies proves there
■ can be a difference in the kind of body one
■ has before the resurrection and the body one
■ has after the resurrection. With the variety
■ and adequacy with which God has clothed
■ all kinds of celestial and terrestrial life, He
■ should be able to provide suitable bodies for
■ those who will share in the eternal order.

Paul's Appeal to Scripture (vv. 45–50)

Paul now sought to support and expand his conclusion. He quoted Gen. 2:7 with some modifications, and then commented on it. "'The first man Adam became a living being'; the last Adam, a life-giving spirit." The first Adam was a man of dust, and because of our relationship to him, we all have a physical body. But the last Adam (Christ) is from heaven, not dust. Because of the believer's relationship to Him, the believer will have a spiritual body.

Therefore, the spiritual body of the resurrected believer will be similar to the body of the risen Christ. Such a changed body will be necessary, for "flesh and blood cannot inherit the kingdom of God, nor does the perishable inherit the imperishable" (v. 50).

- *Paul expanded his conclusion by quoting*
- *Gen. 2:7, where he made a comparison*
- *between the first Adam and the last Adam.*
- *He further concluded that because of the*
- *believer's relationship to Jesus, the believer*
- *will have a spiritual body.*

Triumph over Death (15:51–58)

This is one of the most exalted New Testament passages describing the glorious consummation of God's kingdom. Because the eternal order is not one of flesh and blood, all believers must undergo a transformation when the Lord returns. Those whose death has preceded His coming will be resurrected, while those who survive until He returns will be transformed from the perishable to the imperishable; from the mortal to the immortal.

Paul expressed profound thanks to God for what He has done in Christ and what He is yet to do. Since Christ's Resurrection provides victory over death, Christians have an incentive for unceasing labor to the glory of God (v. 58).

■ *Because the eternal order is not one of flesh*
■ *and blood, believers must be transformed*
■ *when the Lord returns. Those whose death*
■ *has preceded His coming will be resurrected,*
■ *while those who survive until He returns will*
■ *be transformed. When this happens, death*
■ *will truly and finally be "swallowed up in*
■ *victory!"*

QUESTIONS TO GUIDE YOUR STUDY

1. How did Paul refute the Corinthians' denial of the resurrection of the dead? What do we learn from his argument?

2. What did Paul mean by describing Christ as the "firstfruits" of the Resurrection?

3. Paul answered two hypothetical but valid questions regarding the bodily resurrection of the dead (v. 35). How did Paul answer these questions? What lessons did he teach about the resurrection?

4. In this chapter, what do we learn about the nature of the believer's resurrection body?

Paul concluded his first letter to the Corinthians with several instructions and greetings. His chief concerns were (1) providing instructions for the offering for the poor in Jerusalem, and (2) exhorting the believers at Corinth regarding their church life.

In Gal. 2:10 we find the earliest reference to the proposed offering for the poor Christians in Jerusalem. The church leaders in Jerusalem had urged Paul and Barnabas to remember the poor, and Paul expressed an eagerness to help.

RELIEF OFFERING FOR JERUSALEM (16:1–4)

These verses in 1 Corinthians show that Paul was true to his word. Evidently, the Corinthians had written Paul about their participation in the offering for the believers in Jerusalem. Paul responded with some specific guidance. We can see at least five principles of Christian giving in this passage:

1. *It is inclusive (v. 2)*. Each member of the congregation was to have a part in the offering.
2. *It is systematic (v. 2)*. They were to set aside a portion of money "on the first day of every week."
3. *It is proportionate (v. 2)*. Members were to give as they had prospered.
4. *It is voluntary (v. 2)*. In the Jewish system, a temple tax was levied annually upon every male twenty years of age and older. Paul apparently made no attempt to adapt that practice here.
5. *It is administered wisely (v. 3)*. Appointed delegates from the Corinthian church would take the gift to Jerusalem. That delegation would include Paul, if necessary.

- *In response to the need for helping poor believers in Jerusalem, Paul instructed the Corinthians to set aside some money, week by week, so that it would be ready to be taken to Jerusalem.*

PAUL'S TRAVEL PLANS (16:5–9)

Paul stated his intention to visit Corinth by taking a route through Macedonia rather than sailing directly from Ephesus (v. 5). Rather than making a brief visit, Paul desired to spend some extended time with the Corinthians, perhaps even a winter. Three times in this passage Paul used the word *you* emphatically. Its emphasis is even more pronounced in the language of Paul's Greek text of 1 Corinthians:

- "I will stay with *you*" (v. 6).
- "So that *you* can help me on my journey" (v. 6).
- "I hope to spend some time with *you*" (v. 7).

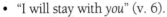

- *These emphases contrasted the Corinthians*
- *with the Macedonians and emphasized Paul's*
- *deep desire to be with the Christians at Corinth.*

Paul also mentioned that he would stay in Ephesus until Pentecost, the Jewish feast that followed seven weeks after Passover. By doing this, he was hoping to take advantage of the opportunity he had to preach the gospel at Ephesus. "A great door for effective work has opened for me, and there are many who oppose me" (v. 9).

- *Paul stated his intention to visit Corinth by*
- *taking a route through Macedonia rather*
- *than sailing directly from Ephesus. His*
- *desire was to spend some extended time with*
- *the Corinthians, perhaps even a winter.*

Province of Macedonia

Macedonia was a crossroads for travel and commerce going north, south, east, and west. The Christian message came to Macedonia through the preaching of Paul, who followed God's vision there (Acts 16:9, 10). The church founded at Thessalonica (Acts 17:2–12) was the recipient of the oldest Christian writing, 1 Thessalonians, which Paul wrote from Corinth after he had preached in Berea and Athens (vv. 13–15). In his travel plans for visiting the Corinthians in 1 Cor. 16, Paul chose the overland route that would take him through Macedonia.

Timothy

Timothy, whose name means "honoring God," was a friend and trusted coworker of Paul. When Timothy was a child, his mother Eunice and his grandmother Lois taught him the Scriptures (2 Tim. 1:5; 3:15). A native of Lystra, he may have been converted on Paul's first missionary journey (Acts 14:6–23). Paul referred to Timothy as his child in the faith. (1 Cor. 4:17; 1 Tim. 1:2; 2 Tim. 1:2). This probably means that Paul was instrumental in Timothy's conversion. When Paul came to Lystra on his second journey, Timothy was a disciple who was well-respected by the believers (Acts 16:1, 2). Paul asked Timothy to accompany him. Timothy's father was a Greek, and Timothy had not been circumcised. Because they would be ministering to many Jews and because Timothy's mother was Jewish, Paul had Timothy circumcised (Acts 16:3). Timothy not only accompanied Paul but also was sent on many crucial missions by Paul.

PAUL'S FINAL APPEAL AND FAREWELL (16:10–24)

The Coming Visits of Timothy and Apollos (vv. 10–12)

Paul mentioned Timothy's forthcoming visit to Corinth and urged the church to receive him as one committed to the Lord's work (vv. 10, 11). Another missionary, Apollos, would also arrive "when he has the opportunity" (v. 12).

Concluding Exhortations (vv. 13, 14)

"Be on your guard." This means to "stay awake, be alert." This word is used for being watchful of the Lord's return, but it can also be a call to watchfulness with regard to the enemy (1 Pet. 5:8) or to destructive influences (Acts 20:31). Here it needs to be understood in view of the following exhortation to "stand firm in the faith."

"Stand firm in the faith." Believers were to *stand* firm in Christ as opposed to *falling*.

"Be men of courage; be strong." Both of these exhortations recall Ps. 31:24, "Be strong and take heart, all you who hope in the LORD." It means to conduct oneself in a courageous way. The Corinthians were to be courageous and strong in the face of the problems that plagued their fellowship.

"Do everything in love." Echoing his theme of chapter 13, Paul's last exhortation to the Corinthians focuses on their relationships. "Everything" would include all Paul had discussed in his letter.

Recognition of Others (vv. 15–18)

In verses 13, 14 Paul provided several concluding exhortations regarding the church life of the Corinthians. Although originally written to the believers at Corinth, these exhortations have application to believers in any age.

Final Greetings (vv. 19–24)

In closing his letter, Paul sent greetings from the Asian churches, with special mention of Aquila and Priscilla, both of whom were beloved by the Corinthians. Paul concluded his letter with a series of his standard greetings and his grace benediction. It ended with a heart-warming benediction to this troubled church: "The grace of the Lord Jesus be with you. My love to all of you in Christ Jesus. Amen" (vv. 23, 24).

■ *In his final appeal and farewell, Paul men-*
■ *tioned Timothy's forthcoming visit to*
■ *Corinth. He concluded by offering several*
■ *exhortations and gave recognition to several*
■ *others for their faithful service in the work of*
■ *the gospel.*

Paul paid a tribute to the household of Stephanas for their faithful service, and expressed joy over the arrival of two men, Fortunatus and Achaicus. We know nothing more about these men. Fortunatus, whose Latin name means "lucky" or "blessed," was probably one of the Roman citizens of Corinth. Achaicus means "one who is from Achaia." Paul related that the arrival of these men "refreshed my spirit and yours also." Whether or not these men were leaders, Paul saw them as worthy of proper recognition.

QUESTIONS TO GUIDE YOUR STUDY

1. What do we learn about Christian giving from Paul's instructions for the offering to the poor in Jerusalem?
2. What might have been Paul's reason for wanting to take the overland route to visit Corinth?
3. From his farewell, how do we know that Paul desired to spend time with the Corinthians?
4. What encouragements for the life of faith might we claim from Paul's concluding exhortations?

The following list is a collection of the source works used for this volume. All are from Broadman & Holman's list of published reference resources to accommodate the reader's need for more specific information and for an expanded treatment of 1 Corinthians. All of these works will greatly aid in the reader's study, teaching, and presentation of Paul's first Epistle to the Corinthians. The accompanying annotations can be helpful in guiding the reader to the proper resources.

RESOURCES:

Adams, J. McKee, rev. by Joseph A. Callaway, *Biblical Backgrounds*. This work provides valuable information on the physical and geographical settings of the New Testament. Its many color maps and other features add depth and understanding.

Blair, Joe, *Introducing the New Testament*, pp. 133–40. Designed as a core textbook for New Testament survey courses, this volume helps the reader in understanding the content and principles of the New Testament. Its features include special maps and photos, outlines, and discussion questions.

Cate, Robert L., *A History of the New Testament and Its Times*. An excellent and thorough survey of the birth and growth of the Christian faith in the first-century world.

Holman Bible Dictionary. An exhaustive, alphabetically arranged resource of Bible-related subjects. An excellent tool of definitions and other information on the people, places, things, and events of the Bible.

Holman Bible Handbook, pp. 686–95. A comprehensive treatment that offers outlines, commentary on key themes and sections, and full-color photos, illustrations, charts, and maps. Provides an accent on the broader theological teachings.

Holman Book of Biblical Charts, Maps, and Reconstructions, p. 98. A colorful, visual collection of charts, maps, and reconstructions, these well-designed tools are invaluable to the study of the Bible.

Lea, Thomas D., *The New Testament: Its Background and Message*, pp. 408–24. An excellent resource for background material—political, cultural, historical, and religious. Provides background information in broad strokes on specific books, including the Gospels.

MacGorman, J. W., *Romans, 1 Corinthians*, Layman's Bible Book Commentary (Nashville: Broadman & Holman Publishers, 1980), pp. 96–153. A popular-level treatment of the book of 1 Corinthians. This easy-to-use volume provides a relevant and practical perspective for the reader.

McQuay, Earl P., *Keys to Interpreting the Bible*. This work provides a fine introduction to the study of the Bible that is invaluable for home Bible studies, lay members of a local church, or students.

McQuay, Earl P., *Learning to Study the Bible*. This study guide presents a helpful procedure that employs the principles basic to effective and thorough Bible study. Using Philippians as a model, the various methods of Bible study are applied. Excellent for home Bible studies, lay members of a local church, and students.

Robertson, A. T., *A Grammar of the Greek New Testament in the Light of Historical Research*. An exhaustive, scholarly work on the underlying language of the New Testament. Provides advanced insights into the grammatical, syntactical, and lexical aspects of the New Testament.

Robertson, A. T., *Word Pictures in the New Testament*, "Epistles of Paul," vol. 4, pp. 68–204. This six-volume series provides insights into the language of the New Testament—Greek. Provides word studies as well as grammatical and background insights into the epistles of Paul.